UNLOCKING THE KEYS TO MAGICK

A Conversation with Franz Bardon Practitioners

The Franz Bardon Community

Falcon Books Publishing Ltd

Published by Falcon Books Publishing Ltd

Cover design and illustrations by Tanya Robinson

ISBN: 978-1-915827-08-1

First Printing: 2023

Printed in the UK

FALCON BOOKS PUBLISHING LTD

St Neots Masonic Hall

166 School Lane, Eaton Socon

Saint Neots

England

PE19 8EH

www.falconbookspublishing.com

Ordering Information:

Please see website for other print options and titles.

www.falconbookspublishing.com

Preface

In this book, we delve into the world of Hermetics as taught by the late Franz Bardon. The Franz Bardon system of Hermetics is a powerful and comprehensive system of personal development that encompasses not only the traditional elements of Hermetic philosophy, but also a wide range of techniques and exercises designed to help the practitioner achieve mastery over the self and the natural world. Through a series of interviews with practitioners of Franz Bardon's system, we gain insight into the powerful techniques and exercises outlined in his books, *Initiation into Hermetics* (IIH), *The Practice of Magical Evocation* (PME), and *The Key to the True Quabbalah* (KTQ).

One of the key elements of Bardon's system is the use of imagination and visualization along with a concentrated and silent mind. Practitioners are taught to use their imagination to create vivid mental images, which are then used to manifest their desires and achieve their goals. Through the development of inner senses, practitioners are able to access and harness the power of the universe to bring about positive change in their lives.

Another important aspect of Bardon's system is the evocation of spiritual entities as practiced in the second of his books PME. Practitioners are taught how to call upon and communicate with spiritual entities, including angels, demons, and other beings from the spiritual realm. This practice is done with the utmost respect and caution, with a focus on ethical considerations and the protection of the practitioner. The work of the first book

IIH ensures that when we enter this realm we are doing so as a deity after the work with our personal god in the later steps of IIH.

Throughout the book, we explore the transformative effects of Bardon's system on the lives of those who practice it. From physical and emotional healing to spiritual growth and enlightenment, the teachings of Franz Bardon have the power to radically change one's life for the better.

Join us as we embark on a journey of self-discovery and unlocking the secrets of magick and the universe through the teachings of Franz Bardon. Through the wisdom and experiences shared by practitioners of this powerful system, we gain a deeper understanding of the principles and practices of hermetics and the potential they hold for personal growth and spiritual advancement.

We dedicate this book to Franz Bardon. Without his tireless work to bring his teachings out into the public then none of this would be possible. Over the last 65 years since his death his work has continued to be a shining light in the world.

May all who read this book be inspired to pursue Franz Bardons teachings with new vigor and share the benefit of your work with the world.

CONTENTS

Introduction

For centuries, the ancient art of Hermetics has been practiced by those seeking to understand and tap into the hidden forces of the universe. At the forefront of this tradition right now in the modern day is the system developed by Franz Bardon, a Czech occultist and magician who devoted his life to studying and teaching the principles of Hermetics.

In this book, we have compiled and updated a series of interviews with practitioners of Franz Bardon's system that were originally published on a previous incarnation of the website - studentsoffranzbardon.com. These practitioners come from all walks of life and share their stories and insights on how they use the principles of Hermetics in their daily lives. These practitioners offer a unique and in-depth look at the power and potential of Bardon's system.

Through these interviews, you'll learn about the various techniques and practices used in Bardon's system, including invocation, evocation, mental travel, and mastery of oneself. You'll also gain insights into the role of the four elements, the use of correspondences and symbolism, and the importance of personal transformation.

Whether you are new to the world of Hermetics and Franz Bardon or an experienced practitioner, this book offers valuable insights and teachings that you can apply to your own journey of personal development and self-discovery. We hope that these interviews will inspire and guide you on your own path of spiritual growth and self-mastery.

andre consiencia

Introduction to Andre

André lives in Moita, Portugal and has been a dedicated practitioner of magic and mysticism for more than two decades. He met Fraternitas Hermetica (an order based on the works of Franz Bardon) while still a minor and had an initiator that stood even after the order vanished. He also has worked with his old initiator for 20 years. He has experience of other magical systems such as AMORC, Order of Michael's Grail (with roots on Dion Fortune), Thelemic Golden Dawn, Astrum Argentum, the Typhonian OTO and the OTOA-LCN.

Interview

SOFB: Thank you for joining us. Please provide us with a brief background as to how you began your Bardon training.

Andre: Thank you for the honor! I had been introduced to spiritism (in particular Allan Kardec and some spiritist centers from Portugal), theosophy (in particular Alice Bailey), some new age movements (in particular the Ascended Masters), to Omraam Mikhaël Aïvanhov and the Great White Brotherhood (not to be confused with the new age approach to ascended masters) and to a first deeper approach to hermeticism in particular through the works of Aleister Crowley and the Golden Dawn in general. I had also known the works of Papus and Eliphas Levi and had some knowledge of the basis of Martinism. I had studied The Mystical Qabalah by Dion Fortune very carefully, making many notes. I had run into all these things due to family issues regarding the so-called supernatural and mediumistic phenomena, and due to my own occurrences. I saw spooks since I could remember, colors in sounds emitted by people coming out from different parts of their bodies, had some memories I couldn't figure out what they were, and was receiving esoteric information in dreams and later while wide awake. I couldn't control or even begin to know what this all was, and I wanted to know, and to have control. It was a blinding need, not only in the sense of a survival urge, which it also was, but an exhilaration, a first feeling of returning home. Then a member from Fraternitas Hermetica, after hearing me speak on Crowley's methods and, on the other side, on so-called ascended masters, sent me *Initiation Into Hermetics* by Franz Bardon. He said Bardon was much better, the appropriation of the ascended masters was mischievous and Crowley's works could definitely go the wrong way. I didn't take that very lightly, so I accepted the challenge of reading Bardon's book to compare.

After reading it, I immediately realized I had outstanding material in my hands, but I went to this person who had given me the book and told him "this is good, but it isn't better". I was still a minor, and had this defiant joviality in me. He didn't argue his case, which I was expecting he would, and it kind of set me off my balance, like a Tai Chi move. During the night I began to argue with myself, a thing he hadn't done, and I decided IIH was probably the best practical book I had gotten my hands on. The next day I decided to test this person, who later became my initiator. I told him "The only problem with this book is that it misses an essential point, it seems to focus more on the work of will-power than on love, yet, only love can balance and harmonize the four elements". He told me he understood that I might choose to think so, but that in his opinion love can only be balanced by will, and that even to love we must first have the power to love. His logic was better, then I started practicing, and he caught me along the way.

SOFB: As you have written some books and written extensive articles I shall keep my basic questions brief. Please explain your preferred approach to VOM and what you see as its ultimate benefit.

Andre: Vacancy of Mind is the cornerstone of IIH. Some might say it is working with the soul mirror, which I can understand. But from my experience, those who can't master vacancy of mind will always get poor results while working with the soul mirror. If one truly masters VOM, all that stands in the way of our belief and determination can simply be erased. Yes, if one is able to fix one's thoughts on a single thought, things that might distract him from this thought stop distracting him. It means such distracting thoughts are not on the front panel of the mind nor are they allowed to come in there, so to speak. But with VOM, there are no front and back panels, you get the whole view, and when thoughts stop coming, that is when you truly know you have control over anything, or better put, over the mind. For instance, when one doubts, and asks while pore breathing "is this true vitality or just my imagination of true vitality?" one is losing vitality. If he removes this thought of doubt entirely, instead of simply not being distracted by it, he immediately starts to build true vitality.

To highlight the importance of VOM, especially in its relation to the Soul Mirror, I like to remember the story of the Three Little Pigs. The big bad wolf is made visible by the black soul mirror, it starts to visibly peek around for its three little pigs, wanting to consume body, soul and mind. Sensations are very unstable, the pig of the body builds his house on them. Feelings are less unstable but still fragile, the pig of the soul builds its house with them. The pig of the mind doesn't build his house on thoughts, mere mental imitations of sensations and feelings, automatisms, he builds his house on vacancy, the stuff of the mind. The big bad wolf of vice sweeps over the house of sensation, it all goes to ashes, but what lived inside sensations survives in the house of feelings. Then it is time for the bad wolf to test the house of feelings, and the soul (that was living in the house of feelings) and consciousness (that was living in the house of sensations and then in the house of feelings) survive in the purity of mind (whose quantity is the vacancy of mind).

Sure, in the story, the big bad wolf doesn't give up when he sees he can't bring down the house of the mind, he tries to enter it from above, and that is when the fire of the spirit hits him.

I hope what I have told here can be understood. One can also bring his attention to the story of Hercules and the Hydra. Before beating Hydra, Hercules was just an heroic personality, he wasn't yet a true initiate. Hydra is the beast of thoughts, Hercules cuts one and two grow back in its place. It is when Hercules lifts the Hydra from the floor that she loses power, and he is able to dominate her. This means to portray that thoughts are but reflections of feelings and sensations, separate the mind from feelings and sensations, and the mind will be silent. Instead of feelings you will find love, the unity of feelings. Instead of sensations, bliss, the unity of sensations.

You can go about Bardon all you like, without VOM, it will all be useless in the end except for the personality and its stimulus.

I have attained VOM through many different methods over time, as some students cannot seem to do it the way I first did it. The way I first did it was very simple, to forcefully expel all thoughts and persist, until only electrical impulses were left, and then stilling the electrical impulses. In the end, there would be void compressing and transbundant light, and once that dynamic state is achieved, it is the other way around, you have to use your will-power to come back. Once this was mastered, I started practicing VOM with my eyes open, and then even while going about my business and while having conversations.

To many this first approach seems to be impossible, so, in my book the Way of Abrahadabra I use the greater capacity people apparently have of fixing their thoughts on a single subject or object. I start with simple thoughts and images, after which come complex images and thoughts, and then I begin to reduce the concepts that fit in the thoughts/images being used. Eventually, you are focusing on the thought and image of a single star in the void black sky. Then, you remove the star, and there is only vital vacancy.

SOFB: Vital Force, some struggle with feeling like they are truly absorbing anything. How can people truly experience a difference in their vitality and health from this pore breathing.

Andre: There are technical answers to this question, but I will use the opportunity to attack a bigger issue I see among students, for there is nothing essentially wrong with the technique exactly how Bardon puts it. A practitioner that intends to finish at least IIH must be prepared to truly believe the impossible. The question is, is he willing to?

He is given the chance to do this very gradually, but still his commitment to the power of his mind must be whole all the while. Take hypnotism for instance, it only works on people who willingly give in to it, that is why Bardon so often writes "the magician will be able to convince himself". He is not exactly talking about reason here. Now, many people fear believing what they thought was impossible because they associate it with the loss of reason and logic, with the loss of control. Nothing of the sort is requested at any time during IIH, on the contrary, reason is essential for the good judgement of how one chooses to use the limitless power of the mind, less the mind destroys itself in the blink of an eye. Power is force, but reason is its rider, and the rider must be sharp in his decisions.

SOFB: Elements, similar to the VF people wonder if they are really getting the element or just an expression of the element. What can they do to meet the true element.

Andre: I repeat the words above, but will now add another hint. Regarding the water and fire elements, Bardon talks of cold and heat, and that one can use a thermometer to test one's success. Being able to physically raise the temperature or lower it is not essential for the effectiveness of the astral fluid, in most cases. The reason Bardon puts it there is, in my understanding, to make it easier for the magician to dissipate any doubts of his effectiveness, that is, to make him believe the power of his imagination, to make him believe the "impossible", or better put, the possible after all. With vitality one can have the same kind of proof by studying if he is more vigorous in his day-to-day or if the sensation is but a fleeting one. Regarding Earth (heavy) and Air (light), I have not tried this, but I suppose one can use a weight scale.

SOFB: Gesture training is not discussed too much. Do you have any insight you can share.

Andre: Gesture training is a form of mnemonics attached to the movements of the body. A gesture attracts a thought, a feeling and a sensation, or is made to attract a particular thought, feeling and sensation by the magician. But more importantly, it is of a martial nature, it brings the thought, feeling and sensation of action into the previously chosen thought, feeling and sensation, so that they become active and, being active, act on their own. This is the power and might of ritual, while its virtue and quality, that defines its success, is also in what makes mnemonics work: harmony, beauty and universal law.

It is said that the rank of an adept can be seen in the perfection of the pentacles he devises, the same can be said about the creation of rituals and gesture sequences.

SOFB: Depth point perhaps one of my favorite areas, a massive stage for students moving from lower steps into some quite strange states of mind. What can you share about the depth point and its significance to our training.

Andre: Here is the second cornerstone, while VOM is the first. If without VOM anything done by the magician is but for the self gratification of personality (no matter how much he arranges his soul mirror to appear pretty in its surface), the depth point allows the magician to go beyond individuality (not to be confused with personality). This is the first time he starts to connect with cosmic power. Even if he is just testing the depth point of an object, he is understanding outside himself, and his consciousness has known the powers of fertility for the first time. This is what brings to the adept his celestial nature. And it is why Bardon's and most hermetic adepts search for the divine powers, while many magical traditions of satanism stick to self deification many times (although there are exceptions) without ever knowing anything beyond their own belly buttons (this is still true when practicing consciousness transference, for any self is the self). Such magicians will be able to create elementaries of elementals, cosmic beings and demons, but won't be met by elementals, angels or even demons.

SOFB Community Questions

SOFB Community: What were your foundational tools and/or experiences that opened up your magical abilities and capacity?

Andre: I am probably not the right person to answer this question. While many start this path to open up magical abilities and capacities, I started in order to control them.

SOFB Community: How would you suggest one fine tune the harmony between their 3 bodies more?

Andre: Art. There is much more to it, but art! Different forms of art, and then art that utilizes them all. For instance, physical exercise is good for the body, it may or may not be called an art, but we are not there yet. Giving oneself to one's emotions is good to know the soul and how it outlasts its objects of attention through feeling. Thinking about things in depth is good to know the crates and surfaces of the mind. Now, dancing is definitely art, it connects the body and the soul. Martial arts is, as the name implies, undoubtedly art, and it connects the body to the mind. Painting connects the mind to the soul. Writing connects all the four qualities of the intellect together. These are mere examples. Performance and theatre can require a lot of all three bodies, failure comes when the three don't act harmoniously. An actor or performer must know what he is doing, the process of what he is doing (cognition), the sense (logic) and underlying intention (will), or he won't even be able to memorize it properly (memory). According to his script, he must have the proper feeling inside (allowing feelings the same dynamism of the mind) and be able to create sensations out of this feeling, in order to transpose it, communicate to the audience and show something on the outside. If one of these elements fail, the show lacks the sublime.

SOFB Community: How do you perceive shadow work and your tips/suggestions for healthy integration of one's inner darkness?

Andre: A man that is whole is always able to communicate with an animal in a way that the animal understands, because he also understands the animal to start with. Because this man is whole, in a way, he is all. Even to such a man, there is use in integrating the shadows, for the harmonious region where he locates his consciousness, the center, is ever knowing, loving and penetrating the circle, and this is the sacred process of life. Not all are ready to do the shadow work consciously, and that is why I consider one of the jobs of the artist to conduct this process in others in a manner that is safe, so that the others can do it through contemplation: when they notice it is about them, sublimation has taken place already. To people who have enough psychological stability to do the shadow work consciously, it is essential for the growth of the soul. When we are young we think the shadows are under the bed or inside the closet, when we are adults we know the monsters are mostly inside us, but if we remove all obstacles (inner beds and closets) and meet them in open fields, they stop being monsters and show the secret of frailty, and in frailty, the tender mystery of love and self love.

As a mere example, I shall tell the story of a particular time when I evoked death. I was obsessed with this feeling of death around me and in my body, I started to have insomnia and anxiety because of it and I came to talk with a friend that is or was the head of René Guenon's organization in Portugal. He told me to drink tea with death and engage in conversation. I did as he suggested, and death was actually very kind, wise and compassionate, she had the most peaceful and healthy counsels to give, and she had been warning me, through the senses, of things that I had been doing unwisely and that I had been unwilling to recognize. From there on, I slept better.

But to go back to how I started (to the animals) a good way to work with the shadows is finding them, understanding them (outer shape, inner shape, silence), moving to their own depth point and transforming them into animals. Then one can start taming them lovingly and they can help us with their power. Shamanism can be a good additional tool regarding this method.

SOFB Community: How do drum-induced trance practices in folk traditions, which facilitate spirit engagement, compare to mental wandering as a means of connecting with spirits in Bardon's system? Why do you think engaging with spirits is less taboo in those folk traditions compared to those following Bardon's system?

Andre: This is a merry topic of which I often think. It is important to note that hermeticism and shamanism are often opposite paths, not in their purpose, but in their approach. While hermeticism acts consciously in every step, and moves the conscious to conquer the unconscious, shamanism works the other way around: it seeks to tap into the subconscious and to integrate it into consciousness. The works are done in a semi conscious state, and the more they are done this way, the more the shaman is a genuine shaman. Mental wandering in shamanism is witnessed, and the shaman controls the journey through intentions he has previously established. He actualizes his acts mostly through the memory of instinct in the spirit, and the less reason interferes, the purer the outcome. Mental wandering in Bardon is of a conscious dynamic, the magician moves by will and reason.

I do not feel that engaging with spirits is a taboo among Bardon magicians, but for some reason it has almost always become a taboo among less tribal and larger civilizations. In those, in which hermeticism spams, men are not used to seeing the world through the lens of animism. They may find special spirits to represent certain principles, or that special things have spirits attached, but in shamanic cultures, literally everything is or has a spirit, and everything is equally special.

SOFB Community: From the different methods to engage with spirits provided by Bardon (e.g., mental wandering, evocation), which one you had most success with? And which one would you see as the most achievable for students coming into PME?

Andre: I had success with both. If by most achievable you mean easier, mental wandering is generally easier, and also a necessity for proper first time evocations. In any case, the magician should not stick with a single method, they are not two ways to reach the same. Evocation can achieve certain things mental wandering cannot, and vice-versa.

SOFB Community: The process of making consecrated tools is always a hot topic in grimoire based traditions. Some claim that every step should be followed to the letter while others are flexible to the point of skipping most of the tools. What's your approach in regards to the preparation and consecration of magical tools when working with PME?

Andre: I remember an occasion when the chamber where Bardon used to work became inaccessible for some reason. During this time, Bardon practiced on his bed silently, with his wife on his side sleeping, one hour before she would wake up. This is an example he gave to his direct students. The important thing is to do the work, and to do it as we can and with what we can. That being said, if there is the possibility, when working with PME, work according to the instructions in PME, for it will maximize the performance. A little bit of the creative genius of the magician should be put into it, I remember Aleister Crowley speaking of carving different wands as the practice of creating, molding and giving life and realization to different dreams.

As an example of personal touch, I have a whip made of two wands (the handle) and a thin rope (binding the wands together) that cuts the air with an hiss when the wands are projected forward. The rope is the light of absolute victory, one wand controls the four elements, and the other the seven planets.

SOFB Community: When working with spirits, do you have a favorite method to keep yourself in check from self-delusions?

Andre: Yes, but it is not present in Bardon's teachings. One must find that part of the astral light that personifies the subconscious of the magician, or the astral light that is being animated by the soul of the magician. By other words, it is simple astral light, in connection with the subtle channels of the magician (being observed by him and moving and expressing itself therefore). The magician must know this "plasmification" very well, in all ways possible, and make it obedient to him, so as not to have it interfere actively in his coming communications, in which it has to become a simple vehicle to original intelligence. When the magician dominates this intermediary, he will probably notice that many of his first acquaintances in the invisible world were different shapes the intermediary was taking.

SOFB Community: With the numerous books, esoteric schools, traditions and religions, how to keep a consistent practice and not become an armchair magician?

Andre: There is no such thing as an armchair magician, a magician either is a magician or he isn't. One who studies magic instead of practicing it is simply a student or a theorist, but the magician, studying in his armchair or writing, is still a magician. There are many schools, traditions and religions, but how can they undermine consistent practice? Hermeticism was built upon this variety itself, it is the work of intelligence. I'm sure variety is no excuse, on the contrary.

SOFB Community: Correct practice of Prayer in our hermetic practices. In the normal use from most people, doesn't it imply that one is weak, and have a lack of what he's asking for, and is asking for a favor, or, begging for the end result ? From what state of awareness are we asking, and from where, and how do we receive the answer?

Andre: Who is "we"? There are so many different kinds of people. What is the "normal use"? Is lacking something being weak? Is asking for a favour always a bad decision? Whoever made this question, and those who identify with it, should answer the question posed: "from what state of awareness am I asking?" Now, remember, the waves in the sea are praying, the winds in the air are praying, the birds are praying, the lion is praying, the poets are praying, and they are all going beyond themselves.

SOFB Community: Can you provide tips or recommendations on memory techniques, such as Memory Palace or Mind Maps, that are suitable for archiving, structuring, categorizing our extensive experiences, associations, analogies, and databases? Have you personally used any of these techniques, or do you suggest any others that might be helpful in this context?

Andre: Yes I have. These are the foundations for building pentacles, so, in addition to them and according to them, build pentacles, build prayers, build astral temples, build rituals, build theatre plays and performances. Engage with them beyond the mind.

SOFB Community: How can we manifest the visual and auditory impressions we receive externally, making them visible and audible to others through means like cameras and audio recorders, without relying on our own voice, body, musical instruments, or software for recreation? Is it possible for current digital lenses to capture outwardly projected condensed images, and can similar technology be used for capturing projected sounds?

Andre: About the right camera filters and fluid condensers, etc, I would go to the gnomes for information. Beyond that, I'm not really in the position to tell with great precision: if your work is intense it will probably be captured. I found that it helps when you are group-working with other capable magicians. At some point you will attune and start seeing exactly the same phenomena, it is a form of trance where the group seems to be on the physical plane still but that the physical plane has jumped to the astral plane. At this moment the cameras will find many anomalies, and cellphones will usually not work for a while, sometimes weeks (when they make it at all) after the magical ceremony. Well, that is according to my experience and that of my former group, years ago.

SOFB Community: Why is mediumship, particularly in physical skills like martial arts, often more physically draining despite a (high and capable) spirit commanding our bodies instead of our minds? How can we offset the challenges associated with mediumship to ensure that the energy expenditure is comparable to performing those skills ourselves?

Andre: First of all, high and capable spirits commanding our bodies will rarely leave it depleted, unless the task they are performing is asking a lot of our bodies' capacity. When this is not the case, you will be refilled, vital, healed and refreshed after they leave. This is not because it is less draining having a new spirit in our body, with all the adaptations the body will undergo, than not, instead, it is because the spirit is high and capable enough to do us this gentleness.

About the last part of the question, channeling is always less demanding than incorporating. You are directly moved by the beings' inspiration, but your mind and soul are still in your body.

SOFB Community: How to go about the process of imbuing a quantity (vital, fluids, etc), with our intention, purpose, ideation? Do we condense firstly the quantity and then put the ideation, inside as a sort of seed, maybe outside surrounding it, other? Do we imagine the final result of our ideation, as a still image, or as a moving gif-image (would certain results need the gif?).

Andre: When working physically, like using fire to burn a paper, burying a potato, as Bardon teaches on low magic, or for the creation of golems, the method uses quantity impregnated by quality. The astral volt uses electric fluid first and then the magnetic fluid, and it builds the quantity upon the quality. Both ways work. Use the perfect still image together with the perfect moving image, according to the principle of the rose and the cross.

SOFB Community: Does the intention, purpose, or ideation always have to be associated with visual images, or can other sensory modalities like inner mind chatter or other sensations be utilized as well? For beginners, how can they recreate the abstract and unfamiliar feelings you mentioned in your article, such as "high cognition, good memory, fertility, feeling of purification," in order to imbue them with their intentions or purpose?

Andre: For the first part: use all you can, the visualization is the creation of a complete world in a complete moment. For the second part, if someone has not a keen mind for the abstract, let him study more magic and philosophy first, and read poetry. The abstract must stop being unfamiliar.

SOFB Community: Do we imagine them as visual images and states of ourselves, and then emotionally engage in those imagined states, so to create those feelings?

Andre: You must search what works for you. Be creative and explore as much as you can. Many different approaches work. For instance, if you are more visual the way you put it is fine, but if you are more sensitive, you engage emotionally and it will give you the visual input. The ideal is to have equilibrium, and to be highly sensitive and highly visual, so that the visual and the feeling don't come one after the other, but simultaneously.

SOFB Community: What are effective ways to cultivate unshakable conviction and faith in our minds ASAP? Does it primarily involve the accumulation of repeated successes, or are there other factors to consider?

Andre: To hurry breeds imperfection. Being always successful doesn't help faith and conviction, because it isn't success at all. Success grows against failure and it requires stamina and perseverance. Being successful enough times to know one can succeed is good for conviction, it gives a certain level of positive certainty to reason and judgement, but faith is another game, it is a state of trance that dispenses all limitations, their conceptions and their judgement.

SOFB Community: Trulkhor, Tummo, Inner heat yoga's, the subtle channels and the vital energies. Do those practices hold any overall value, and do we have equivalent practices in hermetics, if to substitute for?

Andre: Before writing *Initiation Into Hermetics*, Franz Bardon translated Book Four (Liber ABA) by Aleister Crowley into Czech. I suggest the reading of this book (in whatever language), it will make it clear that many foundational exercises by Bardon are based on different forms of Yoga.

SOFB Community: Is it safe to practice pore-breathing (inhaling and exhaling vital energy) in environments with high levels of electromagnetic fields, such as industrial, IT, and tech settings with numerous WiFi, RF, and EMF fields, as well as static electricity? What measures can one take to protect their health in such environments, aside from seeking alternative employment options?

Andre: If someone can breathe there by normal means, he will be able to breathe there consciously. We are always pore-breathing anyway, just not always consciously. The material air is not the idea that we are breathing consciously, and it won't undermine our work. Bardon writes:

"The electrical as well as the magnetic fluid in the human body have nothing to do with the kind of electricity or magnetism we know, although a certain analogy exists."

He adds:

"By normal or unconscious breathing, the body is supplied only with as much elemental substance as is necessary for its normal preservation. Here also the supply depends on the consumption of elemental substance. It is quite different with conscious breathing. If we put a thought, an idea or an image, no matter whether it is concrete or abstract, in the air be inhaled, it will take in the akasha principle of the air concerned and convey it through the electric and magnetic fluids to the air substance. This impregnated air will play a double role when it is conveyed to the lungs through the blood vessels. In the first place, the material parts of the elements are destined to preserve the body; secondly, the electromagnetic fluid, charged with the idea or the image, will lead the electromagnetic air colored with the idea from the bloodstream through the astral matrix to the astral body, and from there to the immortal spirit through the reflective mental matrix."

And...

"Consequently it is quite evident that it is not the quantity of inhaled air that matters, but the quality respecting the idea impregnating the air substance."

Therefore, if we are talking about Bardon, I have no need to elaborate on something he has made clear, and I may use his own words. Nevertheless, if doubt prevails, I suggest the reading of The Complete Works of Swami Vivekananda, Volume I, freely available online.

SOFB Community: Related to Bardon's way of astral separation and travel, are there any ways or practices, to make it more friendly and easier to the practitioner, or will just have to get used to the feelings when re-inhabiting the physical body upon return?

Andre: Better than achieving the result, is cultivating the will-power to make the necessary effort.

SOFB Community: Anything useful, or unknown, about: achieving synesthesia , pareidolia, animating pictures.

Andre: I do not have the knowledge of all that is known, much less unknown, but I know a practicing magician will find it very easy to practice Synesthesia and, in Bardon's tradition, the *Key to True Quaballah* draws on it a lot (not in the sense the usual word implies, that of an involuntary hallucination, but on the conscious fabrication of analogies in the sensory organs of perception). Good instructions are given there.

Pareidolia is a natural phenomena, any child or adult can see shapes in clouds and rocks that go beyond clouds and rocks, and our brain, in reality, does it all the time with whatever object, whether we notice it or not. The brain is an organ of association.

In "The Path of Ipsos Vol I" I write on the subject of pareidolia, taking it to sacred heights:

"The magician is to perceive in everything that non-thing that is endlessly sacrificing itself in order for something to manifest. It can be perceived through its dance. The magician is to stop relating to things, all his deals being with the non thing. From this powerful place of dance and black smoke comes the power of the magician as a shaman. This is his chalice, empty and overflowing."

"When the magician becomes well acquainted with this force it will start to crystallize as non-linearity, or randomness. This means that the magician will understand how between one step and another the large unknown steps in, just as between any two persons, mathematically, every other person can interfere. It is from this state of affairs that the magician will recognize patterns, they have no logic to start with, but they transmit beauty, and therefore they are his first songs of power. Yes, he will start to understand how most of the things in the world have systems of non-linearity, meaning that most of the patterns are shaped by randomness, and it is in this recognizable chaos that beauty lies and, with it, power. What makes the magician capable of grasping true chaos with his ordered brain is the whole being greater than the sum of its parts."

"When the magician shifts his focus more and more into this greater whole, he finally perceives the web that connects any thing to any other thing on Earth, including the stars. The spiral which this web shapes evokes time, but the web itself is outside of time and in a non-ordinary reality. It is outside the circles of time that the magician, as a shaman, is able to contact the spirits."

"It is the random beauty on the outlined patterns of caves, seas, jungles, forests and deserts that make them places of power, places where the non-thing may be recognized in his dance. This concrete form of chaos is named by shamans the lower world. But there is also the non-linear play of light and darkness, of vapors and clouds and the wilderness of crystals, this vague form of chaos is said by shamans to be the upper world. Both have their animistic spirits and the magician is to explore them. The Middle World, where we stand in our ordinary reality, is the place where time goes back and forth and to where things fall from the upper or the lower world when they get lost."

Finally, on animating pictures, a whole book could be written, yet I am giving this interview for students and practitioners of Bardon's works. There is absolutely nothing wrong with that author's indications on the subject. Work, get there, then do it. If you have done all that is asked of you, you will succeed.

SOFB : Thank you for your generous sharing.

CHris

Introduction to Chris

Chris is one half of the 'Knowledge & Conversation' podcast that he co-hosts with well known magician 'Justin B the Magician'. He has been involved in Magick for many years and now in addition to his training within the Franz Bardon system he has also studied deeply the teachings of the Buddha, getting to know these in theory and in practice with a particular focus upon the Vajrayana teachings paying attention to the similarities between the various vehicles rather than just the differences. Though having abundant experience he prefers to see magick through the lens of Kabbalah and most recently committed   to further study of these ancient teachings by joining the Freemasons.

Interview

SOFB: Hello and welcome to Students of Franz Bardon.

Chris: Thanks for asking me to do this!

SOFB: Firstly could I ask you to introduce yourself to the readers, please tell us a little about yourself and how you first discovered Franz Bardon's books and what motivated you to get involved in magic, specifically the Bardon system.

Chris: I'm Chris and I consciously started walking down the magical path about 13 or 14 years ago, but looking back, it seems like I was always meant to go this way. As far back as I remember, I had an inner sense that there was a greater depth and reality to the spiritual than I was given in my mostly superficial Catholic upbringing. I was fascinated by the mystery behind the myths. I started showing creative inclinations very early in life, so to me imagination and curiosity have always been a huge part of who I am. I think it's the combination of those things that lead me to pursue a spiritual life that is based in direct experience rather than through dogma and legality.

To make a long story short, I experienced some trauma in my childhood & teens. That grew into some serious depression, which is a thing that I still deal with today. By my late teens/early twenties, that had blossomed into a hyper materialistic atheism, so when magical things began to happen in overtly shocking ways, I had to investigate it and I had to do it seriously.

What I didn't expect to happen was that the current would carry me to Justin, one of my first teachers, best friends, and K&C co-host, along with a whole group of friends that would become my teachers and magical family so to speak. I was introduced to Bardon soon after. From there I think it was just the right place, right time & right support system that helped me get there.

SOFB: Please tell us about the Podcast 'Knowledge and Conversation'. How did this come about? Did you have any mixed feelings in being so open about your practice?

Chris: Justin pitched the idea of doing a podcast to me a few years ago, but it took awhile for us to figure out what form that would take, learning some of the ins and outs of actually doing one, and getting enough time and equipment to make it. Really though, for me, the seed of the idea came to me when I looked at my occult podcast feed and realized that while there were plenty of podcasts that talked with and about authors and different people teaching, there really wasn't much in the way of magicians sharing the kinds of extraordinary experiences that we all have. The experiences that make magic real to us and worth pursuing. I knew that magicians of all stripes were all around us, I wanted to hear their stories and it seemed the best way to do that is start with our own.

So to tell those stories honestly requires a level of vulnerability that is to me, impossible to fake. I just didn't want to do this at all if I am not being as genuine as I can. That of course meant coming out of the quiet, private life that I had been practicing in for the past few years. It was a hard choice, but so far I'm glad I made it. I've already met some great people that I wouldn't have if I were still keeping my light under a bushel so to speak.

SOFB: In every interview I like to ask some standard questions regarding common sticking points found in IIH:

VOM: Franz Bardon said he expected step 1 to be completed inside of 2 weeks. Do you think this was realistic or the first of many tests of the students 'Will'.

Chris: It can be done, sure, but I wonder how much it matters. If it took you 3 weeks or even 3 months would that matter in a year? Ten years? Thirty years? Would we even remember how long it took? Because that's the scale we're talking about here. VoM is not a thing we do once and quit. It's a profound change that one is attempting to make in their mental habits. It isn't easy, but it's very doable. It's not a race, so why don't we do ourselves a favor; keep working at it and let it come when it comes.

A helpful tip is to get a good workout before, or to practice immediately upon waking, whenever the mind is not already in its usual pattern of behavior, and the body is not going to be complaining from tension or tiredness.

It's also important to remember that this exercise is the third in a series. Some of the folks who get stuck at VOM tend to be skipping ahead a bit, because when we really get it, it's an extension of the other two parts. First we learned to observe the thoughts, which introduced us to an aspect of our minds that could be passive, not partaking of the thoughts, and which is always there. It's the awareness. This should also show us the various ways that thoughts form and appear.

Then we're to focus on one, or to follow one train of thought to the exclusion of anything else. This shows us to a greater extent how thoughts form, and how to diffuse them in order to maintain focus on our chosen thought. If we were really paying attention, we'd notice that eventually we didn't shift as much, but still little thought buds and sense impressions might show up. Memories of childhood, recent events, bits of books and movies. Sensory data from things we're hearing, tensions in the body, emotions and so on. These can be indulged by the awareness to become thoughts or be allowed to arise and pass, never to become a full thought. Eventually, even these go away.

See when we're going about our normal lives, our awareness is hidden from us, it just goes around letting attractive thought buds blossom into full blown thoughts that we inhabit with our awareness, as if it were the sun, and clipping down the ones we don't want to give life to. Our perceptual investment in the thoughts is so profound, we lose the distinction between the impression or bud, the thought itself and us. All the time. It's exhausting when we think about it.

VOM simply extends our newfound still awareness and marries it to the function of eliminating thoughts from occurring. So first we sit in our observer, open, without a thought to concentrate on. We're just there. Ultimately it feels like sitting in a pool and just floating, keeping ourselves and the water still and serene. At first, the thoughts will come. We let them pass. Then the buds show up. We clip them off. They come back. We clip again. It's exhausting and counter productive.

In reality, we don't need to clip them at all. If we let the thought buds dissipate by simply not attaching our awareness to it, it not only goes away... but it's like it never happened. We're just still.

At first, they're going to just keep popping up, but eventually the appearance will only briefly disturb our pool of awareness... so brief we aren't even aware of what it was... then we're starting VOM. When we're still aware, but not automatically attaching to the buds to the degree that we don't even see them.

VISUALIZATION: People tend to spend years here expecting IMAX like results, what is your advice for those on these Step 2 exercises. Did you follow the method from IIH or come up with your own approach?

Chris: I followed the IIH method, but for me visualization wasn't much of a problem. The challenge was discipline, and control over time. Separating out the specific senses was the hard part for me.

That said, I think it's a case of probably trying to overshoot the results. Bardon is trying to get us to have control of our imaginary faculties even when we are doing other things, so that later, when we attempt something like scrying or evocation, we can do it all with ease and still see where we're going! So, we want crystal clear imagination at our command while doing anything else.

VITAL FORCE: Some people can not feel the accumulation, what can they do to feel it more intensively?

Chris: What a great question! Vital force is the root feeling of life itself, so go out and get your blood pumping! Go for a run, or do some yoga. The Wim Hof breathing method is particularly effective too. After finishing these activities, there should be a number of sensations. The flow of blood in the body produces pulsing, rushing feelings throughout the extremities, from the heart outward. That tingle we're feeling right there, behind or inside that is a feeling of LIFE. It's in the stretch of the muscles, the beat of the heart itself.

Yes, We know that's just high oxygenation, but the idea is to amp up the sensations to get a touch stone on it, something to draw on to get us started. (And it is in fact in the air and the blood too!)

Then we can do this with just a few deep breaths, assisted greatly by the pore breathing and skin brushing techniques. If we do this, we should be able to feel the tingling, light feeling. Now if we sit in meditation and bring our whole attention to the sensation to it, it'll grow and intensify in a kind of feedback loop.

We should then let all our senses paint the picture for us then... what does it look like? sound like? Does it get bigger, smaller? What is its relationship to the elements? Don't force it, just let whatever arises do its thing. To me, it looks like golden-white light that buzzes and tingles in little motes that congeal into a fluid of light.

Now, with a bit of luck, we can imagine the sensations and images being drawn in and kind of kindling between our outstretched hands. It builds up a tension, a skin like a bubble of light, and the more we condense it, the brighter and solid it feels. Whether or not you think it works however, make sure to disperse it before you call it quits.

Eventually, the dam breaks and we can feel it everywhere, in everything, because it's there.

ELEMENTS: Getting in contact with what Rawn Clark called the principle of the element can be difficult as at that point the student has no real idea of what this and when it is make believe and when this goal is finally achieved. What are your thoughts here?

Chris: I can't speak for Rawn here, because I'm not familiar with his work, ha ha.

But if I had to hazard a guess, I would say that the principle of fire is that which is at the burning core of the stars, erupts in every volcano and splits the air in the lightning. It is the Fiery passion and will that blazes within. The principle of water is the frozen core of the glacier, the dark pressure of the ocean bottom, the power of the typhoon, as well as the fluidity that allows for ice, water and vapor. It is every year you have ever shed.

In Air it is the gust of a hurricane, thing that carries every sound ever heard, and every word ever spoken. It is the breath in your lungs. In Earth it is the weight of a mountain, the pressure deep with the dark of the Earth that crushes carbon into diamonds. And in you it is the solidity of your own bones that says this is my body.

DEPTH POINT: This is perhaps a big development in the IIH where a big shift has to occur in order to understand the point Franz Bardon was trying to make. Can you comment on the significance of this exercise?

Chris: This is actually a pretty big one. It's deceptive because it occurs only midway through the book, but if done enough times, this can reveal the true nature of reality as pure, empty awareness. It can also unlock a method of gaining access between the magician's mind or spirit and the Akasha or Ein Sof, and the spirit of everything else in existence, and ultimately reveal those things to all be one "thing". It's in hindsight of course that all of this comes together consciously, as a felt reality, but if one masters this, it makes a lot of the following exercises much more potent, on the spirit/akashic levels especially, and really helps bridge the gap on the higher steps.

SOFB: Can you also comment on the difference between the spatial center of a thing and the depth point of a thing.

Chris: The spatial center of a thing is where we can access the objects consciousness, like a pit in a peach. If we drill in deeper, smaller and smaller until atoms swirl around us like distant galaxies, into the akasha, we are in its depth point, where nothingness and beingness hang together as the fundamental paradox of existence.

GESTURE: Not much is ever heard about the application of Gesture training to create our own finger rituals. Has this been a useful part of your training and if so how have you applied these rituals in your training and daily life.

Chris: I use these like crazy. Beyond just using hand gestures for energetic purposes, like assigning them to elements, I use them for whole rituals, cosmic letters, even spirits that I have that kind of rapport with, though I generally don't bother them if I don't need to.

SOFB: If you had to guide someone through IIH is there anything you would change in the way you presented the training?

Chris: I think there's some points that the general tone is too stern or sparse. Most of the problems that I have seen center around the First step's spirit training. That's probably what I would expand on, detailing how the three exercises work together, and stressing the idea that they aren't a thing to be done and that's it, but that it's really the most foundational aspect of initiation.

SOFB: Though of course working through IIH has to have had an enormous impact upon who you are, did this have any overt impact upon your working and public life and how others saw you?

Chris: Absolutely. I am not unrecognizable from the person that I always was, but I am a much more principled, generally happy, empathetic and brave person than I was when I started. My early life was very difficult in many ways, and it would have been far easier to hide from those traumas than deal with them. Bit by bit, layer by layer I am getting better. I am a better father, husband, brother, and friend by every dimension that I can judge. Bardon was instrumental in that growth.

SOFB: We asked earlier about sticking points that some have trouble with but in your rise through IIH did you also come across steps that caused you real trouble? If so how did you get past this and move on?

Chris: Of course I did! I remember having the biggest trouble getting around the second step's spirit training where we separate the imaginary senses. I had always had a pretty active imagination, but never that much control over it. Things would just pop up all bundled together. Ultimately I got around this by allowing it to happen, and then just concentrating on the aspect I wanted, and once I became aware of what it was like, I would try for that experience again. Of course that only carried me so far, but with time and determination, I eventually got the hang of it.

SOFB: How has your magical training aided you in your work within Freemasonry? You mention on your podcast that Freemasonry provided some elements that you were missing from Franz Bardon's system.

Chris: There's a lot to be said here!

Bardon's system is really all one needs for personal development in many respects, but it was written in a way that divorces it from lots of other threads of western mystery traditions. He does it for good reasons, but it presents us with a problem to solve. If we want to understand anyone other than Bardon, particularly defunct groups like the original Hermetic Order of the Golden Dawn, without actually joining reconstructionist versions of those groups, we have to translate it.

Masonry helped me parse the different strands of influence that exist in the GD specifically, but also showed me how rituals devised by such groups operate, beyond what Bardon explains. It would be all too easy to give importance to something that is not relevant except in a masonic context. And this happens a lot. Too many people in the wider occult community are "experts" in massively complex systems that were and in some cases are way more experimental and flexible than we would think. This is how stuff like Chaos magic come about, reinvents the wheel and thinks it owns concepts like innovation, when it was there all along, it's just hard to see from the outside. The benefit of a tradition in understanding how these ideas flowed through time orients us in a way that going it alone just cannot do.

If you know that the base template they are using is Freemasonry, it's easy to see how they made use of that to shine a light on Hermetic, Chalean or kabbalistic concepts in order to bring them into harmony. A good example is just in how we see things like degrees. From the outside, a lot is made about receiving a degree and the spiritual experience of it. In reality, taking a degree is like drinking from a firehose in a magical sense. It's a thing that one studies and comes back to again and again. When all of that understanding matures, it's in the giving of the degree where the magic really happens. In sharing the light of wisdom that one has acquired.

Another thing it taught me was how these things actually function. I went in expecting something very different from what I got. I expected more studious, enlightened folks talking philosophy and esoteric concepts, and it's there but that's only a small part of it, and not even the most important part really. I eventually came to appreciate the role that each little thing, each person played in keeping the organization going.

There's also the ideal of accepting people from differing spiritual backgrounds as equals that I really love. That said, Masonry is an old organization and so it has social problems that need to be addressed, but I think it's still capable of changing and getting better.

SOFB: Do you use any other methods in your work or have familiarity with other systems Eastern Or Western?

Chris: When I started, our group had people doing all sorts of things, and Justin and I both learned a lot from a friend of ours who was a Yogi with a seemingly bottomless knowledge base about everything else too.

I really got into Buddhism for a while as well, and even had the opportunity to spend a year or so with some Buddhist monks who taught me some pretty incredible things. I didn't stick with Buddhism, but I'd be lying if I said that there isn't an influence there.

Over the years, I've also studied a lot of kabbalah. I started with the Hermetic stuff and have been moving more and more into the traditional Hebrew form of it. The funny thing about that is that I can find a lot more agreement in all of Bardon's system with the Hebrew view than the Hermetic, he just incorporates more Eastern and Alchemical vocabulary rather than Hebrew. But in truth, the reason I love kabbalah is that, when approached a certain way, it seems to contain an analogue to virtually every other system that I have been exposed to. Even Bardon's unconventional hermetic ideas have a Hebrew term for them somewhere in a kabbalah text!

Alchemy and Yoga should get some mentions here too. I do a regular yoga routine and combined with Bardon meditation/elemental work it's my typical magic hygiene. Yoga, even as a purely physical exercise makes meditation and astral work much easier.

SOFB: Mental Travel and Franz Bardon's specific approach to Astral travel. How significant were these skills in your development. What I mean here is was your worldview impacted at all after completing these steps in what you experienced upon being successful in the training?

Chris: Over time I learned that the planes aren't discreet islands unto themselves, but rather that they exist on a continuum of experience that can be broken down in various ways; some useful and others less so. Bardon's system is structured very similarly to the Kabbalistic model of the parts of the soul and the four worlds, and that's what the third book is based on, but here what I learned is that the in the thread connecting us from spirit to soul to body is an infinitude of states that is the gateway to our true being, the Ein Sof or pure divinity.

SOFB: How important is it to do the Astral Travel training of Step 9 in the way Franz Bardon explains rather than creating some sort of Astral double or illusory body without the Mental/Astral separation before integration? As much of what is read about all seems to point to practitioners taking the later approach and not the former challenging approach of Bardon.

Chris: I think Bardon and I would both say to learn multiple methods of doing anything, provided they are effective, which time would reveal to the practitioner if it's viable or not.

Personally I used Bardon's more than any other, but over the years it's gotten very streamlined. I can effectively do it by imagination and will alone now, but most of it's like that these days, just as Bardon promises.

SOFB: PME and KTQ. What have these books brought to your practice? We know these are very private but would appreciate anything you can share about these works and the experiences they bring.

Chris: Evocation isn't something that I do a whole lot of, but Bardon's theoretical framework applies to basically any grimoire that I can think of. It's formed the basis for how I interact with spirits of any stripe.

KTQ is another example of using the text to build a personal practice for me, but it's more about how Bardon fits into the wealth of kabbalistic material out there. Go read Sefer Yetzirah if you haven't.

There are so many stories I could tell... and that's what the next episode of the podcast is all about!

SOFB: Did the way you saw IIH change after moving onto these books? In that it was preparing you for something?

Chris: Yes absolutely! *The Key to the True Kabbalah* is the book that kicked off a decade of Kabbalistic study that doesn't seem to be ending any time soon.

SOFB: Lastly is there anything else you would like to add that you feel is important for students of IIH.

Chris: Try not to rush through it, especially since it isn't a race. It's going to be a thing you'll do for years to come if you're meant to. Also, don't be afraid to let intuition help you out when you get stuck. It's very possible to "dry out" many of the exercises by not allowing your mind to show you the way toward accomplishing a task.

And trust in the divine providence to help you out when you need it. Tat Tvam Asi!

SOFB : Thank you for your generous sharing.

YOGIC ENGINEERING

Introduction to Yogic Engineering

Yogic Engineering – is the creator of the blog called 'Yogic Engineering'. From posts on that blog and indeed in the interview below you will see that he is a practical individual who is interested in results not magical fantasy. He is a private individual hence us using the name of his blog in this interview as his name. In his own words from his blog:

After almost 30 years of experience in yogic and meditative practice, a long career in government and way too much time spent in out of the way places I am now at the point I feel comfortable sharing what I've learned. My experience with yogic practice started in the late 1980's. Over the next 30 years, I've studied Surat Shabd yoga, the Taoist yogic practices, Vajrayana Buddhism, and finally Hermetics. While I have studied Tai Chi, Bagua, and Xingyi at various times my martial practice mostly centered around firearms via CQB. Frankly, better teachers exist for all of those things. My unorthodox career has allowed me to road test a lot of the yogic practices under circumstances that most people do not have access to. I'm now at the point where I can share some of this with you.

Interview

SOFB: Thank you for agreeing to this interview. Please tell us a little about your background, training prior to IIH and how you came to discover Franz Bardon and his teachings.

YE: Multiple Taoist and tantric Buddhist trainings, Kundalini Awakening via Glenn Morris methodology, some Native American training from American Southwest and some Golden Dawn work via the lineage of John Michael Greer over a 20 year period. I had read the books earlier, but they were inaccessible to me. Too wordy and technique was not spelled out in a modern (i.e. " bullet points") format. A few years went by then I found out about Rasmus giving a seminar near where I was living and crashed it.

SOFB: There are many students working on IIH and have been 'stuck' in the early stages for many many years. Whether that be VOM or Visualization, what suggestions do you have for these students to help them progress in their studies and what do think is the cause of so many getting stuck?

YE: Multiple traps are built into the book to derail training.

The biggest of which is the insistence to not progress to the next level before finishing the previous one. Remember: The perfect is the enemy of the good. Follow-on exercises actually reinforce earlier work and vice versa.

Second, the book is poorly organized. For example, you need to learn the electric and magnetic forms immediately after learning how to generate vital energy. Electric and magnetic split into the elemental forms, not the other way around. I've also had students experience non-dual light just from aggressively working the magnetic and electric in equal amounts.

Third, the book does not clearly delineate an effective form of body training. For example, the easiest way to train electric/magnetic is using posture and an expansion of the ligaments/tendons of the body. Without a good body training method, it is difficult to generate the various energies strongly enough to get the proper sensation.

If I were on my own and had no one to work with, I would do the following:

First, take up Olympic weightlifting. The whole body movements in this both build and integrate the ligament and tendon network in the body. This is going to make your energy work much stronger. Notice, I did not say bodybuilding or CrossFit.

Second, get your bodyfat below 15% if a man and down to around 20% if you are a woman. Vital force forms your base in the early stages of training. If you are obese, this isn't going to work well. I am agnostic as to diet, but do keep in mind that a vegetarian diet increases sensitivity while an animal protein heavy diet increases throughput and power. Just because the energy "feels" strong doesn't mean it is strong. Likewise, if you cannot sense energy, you cannot manipulate it. Sensitivity and power exist in a continuum in the beginning, but you need both to get anything done.

Three, map out all of the skills in IIH and put them onto a spreadsheet. Next write each technique down step by step. You do not need all of these either. For example, I don't do the pendulum or black/white mirror exercises and have never taught them. Likewise, many of the tool based exercises while convenient are not necessary for development. At the end you should wind up with between 50-60 skills. Line these up in a row one after another.

Get a string of beads. Next practice one skill after another for five minutes each using the string of beads and a digital clock. The whole series should take about 3 hours. Add in your tendon training work and call it four hours. If you do this twice a day for a year, you will have mastered the whole book. I didn't do it this way myself, but that would be the most efficient method for a solo practitioner.

I don't work with the black and white mirrors for one simple reason: human beings are bad observers of their own behavior.

It is made worse by the fact that as of 2019 we live in a society that gives children participation trophies in sports, fat acceptance is apparently a real thing, and people are constantly reinforcing bad behavior by telling others how great they are at something when in fact they suck. The world of southern Germany and the Czech Republic where Franz Bardon lived, and most importantly grew up, in the 1920s and 1930s was very different in this regard. People constantly told you, particularly elders in a position of authority, what you were good at and, most importantly, what you were bad at. People of this era knew without question what their strengths and weaknesses were.

I do not teach, or practice, the mirror exercises as it typically results in people manipulating what they think their good/bad qualities are. Which explains a lot of the strange, and imbalanced, behavior this community exhibits. People are literally brainwashing themselves. Generally, it results in people strengthening the parts of their personality they like. Simply put, very few people in this work seem to come to terms with the fact that, as people, we just are not that smart.

The good news is that this is not necessary in the end. Every time you work with the sense gate exercises (sight, sound, smell, etc.) you are working with elemental associations in the body. Every time you work with the elements you are working with the qualities of omniscience, etc. If you establish magical equilibrium often enough, it feeds back through your system and things balance. All without the risk of actively unbalancing yourself. The whole process on a raw level takes a few months and works itself out over a period of several years. Which is why I stress the need to establish equilibrium frequently throughout the day.

SOFB: Looking at IIH what would do you believe to be the main skills taught and how do you address these skills in your teaching of students? Do you follow the book to the letter or have you found more efficient methods?

YE: The three crucial skills are body training, sensory gate exercises and the ability to focus the mind.

Body training, as already stated, isn't really covered in the book beyond some general information on "asana". Body exercises strengthen and integrate the ligament/tendon/fasciae in the body, which allows you to run more energy in a much stronger manner through the body. It also allows a practitioner to ground more subtle energy into the physical.

The sensory gate exercises allow you to detect and manipulate the various energies. This is largely what "energy work" and chi gung is about. It involves sensation, perception and emotion. You don't need to do the sensory gate exercises to move large amounts of energy. A good powerlifter, or martial artist, is a dynamo of energy that will almost always overwhelm a meditative practitioner. You just need to be strong. It is also why the best practitioners historically almost always came from the warrior caste. You do need the sensory exercises to focus what you are doing and to provide a controllable application.

The focusing exercises allow you to shut down outside distractions and reinforce the will. By simply focusing enough, you can often bore your way through many forms of resistance. Raw force of will has put men on the moon, raised empires, created billionaires and generally been responsible for every significant innovation in human history. And if that isn't enough, once you die and no longer have a physical body, focusing mental energy is apparently how you build power in the afterlife.

As such, the three most important exercises in the books are: the asana exercise, vital breathing via building the ball, and the single pointed focus exercise. If you can do these three things, you can unlock the rest of the book.

With my students, I start with "building the ball" which is a take on vital breathing where you build a ball of vital energy between the hands. When they can do this, they can sense vital energy and manipulate it. Then I teach them the electric/magnetic exercises via fasciae work. Finally, I teach them the single pointed focus exercise where you reproduce an object in you mind. A pen works well for this. All of that takes about four to eight hours depending upon the individual.

About 85% of what I teach, excluding the body training, is from the book. Everything else is easy to understand if you have mastered the skills in the book. And that is Bardon's biggest gift to all of us. The skills in IIH represent what most people would develop if they stayed at a practitioner's temple in Asia over the period of about 18 months. They essentially represent your basic training in the meditative/yogic arts. The advantage here is that you do not have to give up your personal freedom, become a monk and live under the construct of that system. The downside is that no one is supporting your practice.

Three additional items are worth mentioning that do not come from the book that I teach and find to be invaluable. The releasing techniques, breath retention and the orbit technology. The first two are necessary additions and the third is a nice to have.

The releasing techniques as covered in the Sedona Method (https://www.sedona.com /Home.asp) are a major addition to what I teach. This allows a practitioner to quickly discharge emotional flare ups, control pain and get rid of energetic excesses as they sometimes form when training other skills within Bardon's system. It is also something that can be taught as a standalone technique that anyone can use. The Sedona Method people get a little carried away with this technology, but it both works and is very effective.

Breath retention work solves the issue of people becoming overly energetically empathetic that makes living in crowded cities a problem. It re-establishes the proper functioning of the sphere of sensation around the body (what the Chinese refer to as your wei/guardian chi) and has a general tonifying effect upon the health as well. Classical pranayama works well, Tao Semko teaches a form of Trulkhor (taosemko.com) that is good too and my favorite system is the Emei Sudden Enlightenment School as taught by Linhai at sacredjourneys.org.

Finally, I have found that awakening the kundalini by using the orbit technology developed by Dr. Glenn Morris provides a density to a practitioner's power that other forms of development lack. Dr. Morris is deceased, but his two lead students (Santiago Dobles and Tao Semko) have further refined his work over at https://kundaliniawakeningprocess.com/blog/

SOFB: You have a very practical down to earth approach in your writing, that these skills are outcomes of the correct input. So would you say that if the student does enough input then they will get the results regardless of their moral compass? You mention on your blog having met many highly skilled cult leaders and criminals. If this is the case, what then is the relationship between ennoblement of the spirit/moral thinking with our progress in hermetics?

YE: Absolutely.

No one says you need to be a good person to drive a car or cook a meal. It is almost taken for granted that high level performers in most fields are complete assholes in real life. Their excellence came at the expense of something else. Regarding the moral compass question, why would it be different in meditative/yogic practice? I will add it is harder to focus your efforts when you are doing drugs and screwing around.

The ennoblement of the spirit really falls into two main functions as I've seen it practically manifest. First, serious, long term practitioners gradually lose their bad habits. Notice I said gradually. It can take years. You stop smoking, because it negatively impacts your ability to split vital and astral energies. Then you stop watching porn, because it makes your vital energy take a dump. Five, or six, years and several bad habits lost later, you are a boring guy who does nothing but practice and work like a demon.

Second, the mental stability resulting from frequently establishing equilibrium gives you a pause before you do something bad. It becomes that voice in the back of your head that says, "doing a bunch of coke and banging all of these hookers is a waste of time." But that is all it is. You still have freewill.

And that is the most dangerous part of evil men who practice. They are actively, and often dispassionately, doing bad things, because they want to do them. While karma gets the final vote, that vote may be decades away.

The cult leaders, rapists and thieves I've known who were into this stuff did have a couple of interesting trends in terms of their working lives. First, they routinely go through these build, and bust, cycles where whatever they are doing builds up rapidly and then at some point implodes. Two, they have no real friends. No matter how well they magic other people up, sooner, or later, their real personality comes through and they are alone again. They do have followers though. And these can be more dangerous than the cult leader for your personal safety.

As for me, I'm not really into the cult thing. Way too much work. As a friend mentioned when watching one sex cult leader at work said, "Just watching this guy keep all of these bitches in check is exhausting."

SOFB: If you do not mind sharing how have the skills developed in your hermetic journey assisted you in your work in dangerous locations around the world?

YE: I'm going to include my other meditative/yogic work in this answer as that will cover the more physically demanding/dangerous periods of my life. Completely invaluable. I would be dead without it.

From the enhanced awareness that comes from the sensory exercises, I avoided many otherwise fatal encounters. Your body will give you about a ½ to 1 ½ second lead on fatal activity when properly trained. Some say this can grow up to 5 seconds. This is more than enough to get the jump on the bad guys or simply move out of the way. I missed two suicide bombings in Jerusalem by less than 5 minutes and was literally around the corner from a third that injured over 100 people.

The more ligament/tendon focused exercises gave me a physical durability that is unparalleled. Not many people can walk away from a parachute canopy failure with a broken back (from gold bell training). Accelerated healing to the point that broken bones would heal in a couple of weeks and deep lacerations in days (condensing techniques merged with running the orbits and a young healthy endocrine system). Tendon training also results in an odd form of speed over short distances. Under the right circumstance people have told me I blurred when moving. Neurological response and speed are off the charts. Not even a hint of PTSD. I get angry about the things I wasn't allowed to do, not the things I did.

The more internal work I did, the easier the ritual work got. Once, I even consecrated a flashing talisman to Saturn in a Conex in Afghanistan. It worked great. Of course, I blew out an entire bank of generators the next morning. Akasha really doesn't mix well with power generation equipment. I ran it for 90 days straight.

SOFB: Now let us look more specifically at certain exercises/Skill sets in the early steps.....can you give a little tip in the following areas or share some insight on these stages.

VOM: Franz Bardon said he expected step 1 to be completed inside of 2 weeks. Do you think this was realistic or the first of many tests of the students 'Will'.

YE: I don't see why not. You can learn the basic techniques in an afternoon with a good instructor. But, as I said earlier, the perfect is the enemy of the good. Practice a group of techniques in a kind of loop and everything goes much faster. Also practicing with a group of friends accelerates things. Keep a good journal after each practice and review it once a week.

VISUALIZATION: Are we expecting too much here? Some have said it is more about the ability to focus on the thing for 10 mins than seeing the thing.

YE: Five minutes is adequate for the first book. If you can work up to 30 minutes, as another friend's school requires, the elements really come alive. I was staring at paint flecks on a wall for up to 20 minutes at a time as a kid. So, this was never really a personal challenge. I was a weird kid.

VITAL FORCE: How do we know we are truly breathing in VF? If we believe we are does it make it so? As FB always says it is about our Will and Imagination and that the entirety of IIH is built upon this.

YE: Inhale through the pores of the skin into the center of the body. Exhale thru the palms of the hands visualizing a ball of energy resting between your hands. Play with the ball. Make it bigger. Make it smaller. Rotate it. Rub it over your forearms. Over time, maybe as little as a few minutes and no more than a week, you will begin to feel the boundary layer at the edge of the ball. This is vital force. Once you can do this, it is a matter of splitting the energy into different forms for everything else.

It isn't about will and imagination.

It is about sensation.

Tactile learning is the fastest in my experience. Mainly because our sense of touch is the least degraded of the subtle senses. In many ways, you have no sense of touch without the subtle aspect.

ELEMENTS: Same as for VF, can we easily fool ourselves into thinking we are achieving this? Or does fooling ourselves actually make it so. Additionally, how do we distinguish between our external behavior and the internal element actually transmuting as we tackle our mirrors?

YE: If you have done tendon training the energy manifests much stronger than without it. Additionally, train the mother letters of the Kabbalah from day one. Fire is Sch, Air is A, Water is M and Earth is A umlaut. By doing it in a Kabbalistic way it manifests much stronger and allows you to practice three-part (color, sound, sensation) concentration from the beginning. It takes 10 hours with each energy to generate them cleanly. And 100 hours to make it strong. Always counterbalance in the same session with the opposite (fire and water, air and earth). If the energy becomes unbalanced you will know it. Air to excess, for example, results in an asthma like attack. It is neither subtle nor pleasant. When you get it, it is physical. Not imaginary. Without tendon training work, this is hard to do.

DEPTH POINT: Could you explain the difference in experience with entering the depth point of a thing and entering into the spatial center, as sometimes it can be easy to misinterpret this.

YE: Depth point training was never hard for me. That said, I always paid a lot of attention to establishing equilibrium in the beginning multiple times per day and every time before I tried techniques like this. To the degree I can give advice, establish equilibrium firmly before trying to access the depth point.

SOFB: After IIH the journey continues in PME and KTQ. Now I know these are very personal experiences but wondered if you were able to share anything regarding your experiences with beings of PME and the impact beginning KTQ has had upon your hermetic training.

YE: First, the books are out of order. Do KTQ before PME.

I personally have a heretical, and unpopular, view on the issue.

The planetary meditations are essentially a trap. They really only exist into the astral/mental realms.

What happens is a spirit grabs ahold of a specific frequency of energy and proceeds to be a specialist in that energetic form. In many ways this represents a bottom up organization of the information. The advantage of working with a spirit is that they can tune an practitioner's system/body in an almost digital manner to that frequency, disable internal safeties meant to protect the body from projecting too much, and provide much useful information regarding how to use the energy. In exchange, they get to express themselves in the physical world through you.

Understand this point.

They will manipulate your senses and thoughts with greater strength the longer you work with them. This represents an abridgment of your free will. If it is a mutual goal, then it is potentially worth it as you can progress with something using far less effort/quicker than doing it on your own.

But you get worked in the process.

And these are creatures that gave up enlightenment for the pursuit of power. Think about this.

They also get replaced from time to time and are generally incapable of recognizing the truth when they see it. Frequently they are completely amoral and do not understand the limitations of the physical body.

Once I invoked an entity that specialized in qing gong/light body skills. The next thing I know I'm bounding three feet into the air and bounced off a puddle of water. I thanked the spirit and sent him home. My spine hurt for three weeks afterwards.

Physical evocation results in less mental manipulation, but you cannot really tune into a given frequency this way. And it can be physically dangerous. Look at the works of Dr. Steven Skinner for more information on how to do this.

Also, a lot of the problems people encounter regarding the planets is closely related to their experiences in life. The first four planets are fairly universal in terms of human experience. So, any adult can access these. After the Sun things become highly contingent on personal experience.

For example. If you have never been to war, Mars is going to be very harsh. In many ways this is like obnoxious music being played outside a restaurant to keep the bums away. It will get louder until you get inside. And if you have no personal experience with it, it will come across as very confusing and harsh. For me, it was all about martial brotherhood, loyalty, honor and fitness. Frankly it was quite pleasurable. I've spent the better part of a decade deployed during my life and been in half a dozen conflicts. We fought some of the most evil human beings walking the face of the planet. You enjoyed killing them.

Likewise, if you have never run anything, or have never been in charge of an organization, then Jupiter will be unpleasant. If you have never sat in judgement over another human being, Saturn is going to be difficult.

Finally, if you really look back into the distant past most sources maintain that the planets are ultimately malevolent regardless of which one you are dealing with, while the stars are beneficent. Food for thought. I strongly recommend Gordon White's book Star Ships for information regarding early human history, the transition from stellar to planetary meditations and it is a good background reading on how academia is not your friend. He is a chaos magician out of the UK, and the book is researched extremely well.

The letters represent a top down organization of information, and power, regarding fundamental forces/building blocks in the universe. They are also unintelligent and essentially blind forces, but you do not get manipulated either. So, accessing specific information is really difficult without looking around a lot. A hammer doesn't tell you how to use it. Neither does a brick. The parallel is similar here. Bardon did us all a favor when he scoped the main issues associated with each letter at a given level of existence. His book was remarkably incomplete in some ways as well.

The organ associations are all screwed up. Do not put the letter K in your left ear. The letter R contains many surprises.

I suspect his secretary constructed the book from notes left over after his death. Maybe a rough draft at best.

SOFB: Lastly is there anything else you would like to add about Hermetics or training in general? Any news on the book you mentioned you were writing on your blog?

YE: Come hell, or highwater, my book will be published in the fall. It is slowly coming out of publishing purgatory and I will announce it here. First as an e-book and later as a print on demand. These will be low cost. Finally, if enough interest is gathered, I may have a limited print run done on acid free material and leather bound. This will be very expensive, but it will be personally signed.

I am working on a training program for conducting the stellar meditations. Sometimes these are referred to as the "Trials of Heracles". That should take another year or so. I am still figuring out some of the associations

A friend is working on a video instruction program for the IIH incorporating much of what is discussed here. It should begin its rollout around the time my book is published in the fall. It will contain much of the supplementary material discussed here. I will likewise make an announcement when that becomes available. It will reorganize some of the material from the first book as well to speed development and will be available on Vimeo for download.

Finally, always remember that no mind/body disconnect exists. What we do is physical, practical and tangible. The engineering works even if the science is crap. The difference between theurgy and thaumaturgy is in the application.

A Roman road builder didn't need to know materials science to build a road that carried a given load using specific materials. If you exceeded his known limits though, he had no idea what was going to happen. It is no different with our work.

SOFB: Thank you for your time and amazing information you have shared with us.

Scott Turner

Introduction to Scott Turner

Scott lives in Chile with his wife and three children. He teaches classes in visual effects in a small art college and works on commercials for television.

Interview

SOFB: Firstly could I ask you to introduce yourself to the readers, please tell us a little about yourself and how you first discovered Franz Bardon's books.

Scott: I convinced my wife to let me go try this ayahuasca stuff with the local shaman. I ended up taking it very regularly during which my awareness of magic was awoken. I read hundreds of magic and religious books in that time trying to figure out what was going on. I had downloaded one of those huge archives of hundreds of books and I actually read a lot of them. I kept seeing IIH but for some reason skipped over , until one day I opened it and read it all in one sitting more or less. I connected with it immediately and found it comprehensive and easily understandable but I wasn't prepared for some of the events which were to come as I delved into this magical knowledge.

SOFB: In every interview I like to ask some standard questions about sticking points found in IIH:

VOM: Franz Bardon said he expected step 1 to be completed inside of 2 weeks. Do you think this was realistic or the first of many tests of the students 'Will'.

Scott : Probably not a realistic timeline to master but it doesn't mean you shouldn't forge ahead and also return to it later to reconsider under the lens of more experience.. For example, true thought control can be quite difficult to achieve, as is true self knowledge. Perhaps sometimes we may think we have achieved both of these things down only to realize later that we didn't really know what we were doing.

VISUALIZATION: People tend to spend years here expecting IMAX like results, what is your advice for those on these Step 2 exercises. Did you follow the method from IIH or come up with your own approach?

Scott : I had success with most of the visualization exercises after a lot of practice, but for me it was Robert Bruces 'Energy Work' book. Once I had mastered that I came back to Bardon with newfound enthusiasm and found it very easy.

VITAL FORCE: Some people cannot feel the accumulation, what can they do to feel it more intensively?

Scott : I've tried to teach this and I would say 95% have difficulty feeling accumulation, although I think it's a difficulty in just believing it might be possible and also knowing what to look for as a sign that it's beginning to work. Essentially its about the accumulation of the focus of consciousness. For me when i started, it felt like I was 'just imagining' things . I felt some kind of underlying force but i didn't know how to connect with it and this was after a couple of years of following various paths from Bardon to Regardie's middle pillar. I was having events occur but i didn't feel control over them. My big breakthrough came after an Amazonian kambo frog medicine ceremony in which the Hindu-oriented shaman invoked Shiva and I suddenly felt a field of energy around me which is still with me. The next day i discovered the book 'Energy Work' by Robert Bruce which somehow dropped into my lap at the right time and which I consider to be the 'Accumulation for Dummies' guide. It's a good supplementary detour for people have difficulty with Bardons techniques. A week after I read that book and implemented the ideas, kundalini shot through my crown chakra in a spectacular mystical event which I could only compare to a DMT experience where I met Shiva and Sathya Sai Baba in some kind of temple with jeweled elephants. I just watched in amazement. This was a mind blowing event. Of course without that energetic initiation by the shaman that book might have just been another book, but with the newly found awareness of energy which was swirling round my body every word of the book seemed like an amazing revelation. Imagining energy accumulating in the body was suddenly an orgasmic experience. Even now if I imagine energy accumulating in say my little finger, the sensation of bliss I get can only be compared to sexual bliss in my little finger. Its crazy.

So even though Bardon cautions against mixing paths or jumping ahead - and I took those cautions very very seriously at first because I made many costly and deeply frightening mistakes when I started - my view now is you have to feel it out for yourself. You will find yourself being guided to the right places when it is time for you.

I can confirm that mixing traditions can be very dangerous. MY experiences with Amazonian shamanism came before I discovered Bardon. When the 2 collided, I thought I was going completely nuts. It was still worth it.

ELEMENTS: Getting in contact with what Rawn Clark called the principle of the element can be difficult as at that point the student has no real idea of what this and when it is make believe and when this goal is finally achieved. What are your thoughts here?

Scott : I don't think the goal is ever finally achieved. This is an ongoing process of reconsideration and purification of consciousness which allows us to continually understand at a deeper level. Again supplementary material can be of great value. The free book 'Tattva Shuddi' From Divine Life Society has excellent insights into the nature of the elements. I had great difficulty connecting with the earth element but was guided to greater understanding of it through studying tarot...specifically Jodorowsky's AMAZING book 'Way of the Tarot' And William Grays work 'Inner Traditions of Magic'. When i started realizing that the materialization of divinity is really what the earth element is about I was able to visualize earth in a different way, and low and behold in Step 9 of IIH Bardon himself points in the same direction when he talks about infusing the elements with divine qualities. So sure you can imagine earth as the physical material of earth and sand or whatever, but your missing the point. It should be visualized IMO as the manifestation of the omnipresence of God manifested in physical reality.

DEPTH POINT: This is perhaps a big development in the IIH where a big shift has to occur in order to understand the point Franz Bardon was trying to make. Can you comment on the significance of this exercise?

Scott : The 'depth point' is a way of verbalizing non physical reality and encourages the mind to drop below physical appearance. In some ways this is analogous to another of Bardons ideas to imagine that there is a soul looking through the physical eyes. At first this is an imaginative practice, but the imagination is greatly misunderstood. The imagination is a technological interface. This is made clear using ayahuasca. My experience is that you can only truly connect with it through long hours of meditation upon energy and elements. Whereas my initial experiences with meditation were sad and unproductive, that all changed after that energetic initiation. It was easy to meditate for 4 hours because it felt so incredibly good physically. It was 4 hours of bliss and i never wanted it to stop and then of course I noticed layers of awareness peeling away showing me the way to higher consciousness. You have to seriously engage with meditation to advance in my opinion. Even using medicines like ayahuasca, while they show you the way, you don't really have the understanding how to achieve the same states unless you involve yourself in prolonged meditation.

SOFB: Also can you comment on the difference between the spatial center of a thing and the depth point of a thing.

Scott : Bardons comments on Archimedes became amazing to me because I found that being able to focus on any point became a gateway into other dimensions as the layers of physical illusion slipped away. THIS was the mystery of the 4th dimension revealed. I suppose in some way I am lucky because a lot of this was not the result of careful consideration and meditation upon Bardon, but because of all the Amazonian medicine I had done opening up my awareness wider than I thought possible. But also there are various layers of consciousness you have to move through to get to that stage in a controlled meaningful and non frightening way. Starting by ruminating on what a depth point might mean to you might be the place to start. Start by allowing your mind to move back and forth between spacial/physical and depth, however you imagine it. Ponder the differences. Don't try and imagine what Bardon meant, try to use your intuition to discover where your own mind leads you with that idea.

In its own way this is a form of meditation because your mind is focused completely on this play between spatial and depth.

GESTURE: Not much is ever heard about the application of Gesture training to create our own finger rituals. Has this been a useful part of your training and if so how have you applied these rituals in your training and daily life.

Scott: My development has run parallel with IIH but not completely. I played around with gestures at one point but wasn't really connecting. So I moved on. My focus has really been on the exploration of internal energy and I have only recently begun exploring the projection of energy from the interior to the exterior. Also, I have avoided more ritualistic applications because I didn't want to make any mistakes. I made many mistakes as a result of being elementally imbalanced when i started. These were VERY dangerous mistakes. Ritual implies an objective or a magical intention and I have taken a more neutral meditative approach generally to avoid trouble. Plus I don't really have any intentions other than knowledge.

SOFB: Though of course working through IIH has to have had an enormous impact upon who you are, did this have any overt impact on your working and public life and how others saw you?

Scott: Take something as simple as the mirror of the soul which asks us to change specific aspects of who we are - To truly consider negative aspects of who we are and reveal them to light. Choose only one aspect, says Bardon, and work on that. That has had profound effects on the way I perceive myself and also upon my marriage and family. The question seems to be whether or not you can truly accept what you perceive as darkness within yourself. Often what happens is our view of what is darkness is wrong. The things we view as darkness are often not the problem. The problem is our projection of negativity onto the behaviour or quality and from where does that emerge. Why are we projecting negativity? This is a key issue in becoming elementally balanced. I work in an art school where probably 99% of the staff has taken ayahuasca, so my public changes were very accepted.

SOFB: We asked earlier about sticking points that some have trouble with but in your rise through IIH did you also come across steps that caused you real trouble? If so, how did you get past this and move on?

Scott: The only steps which really matter at first are Pore breathing and Inhalation of elements. If you can't do this nothing else works. I found it difficult to visualize at first until that energetic initiation, but there are very good supplementary materials available too. Mantak Chia's 'Bone Marrow Nei Kung' is in many ways the same practice on steroids and was very helpful as was Robert Bruce,s 'Energy Work'. Granted some of these have a different approach. For example, Robert Bruce focuses on chakras which at first glance might seem quite a different practice. But the chakras are elemental repositories and meditation upon them also produces elemental balance. I found chakras to be much easier to work with at first and eventually augmented my chakra meditations with pore breathing and a more Bardonian approach. Another good supplemental practice is Nidra Yoga which also moves consciousness around the body which approximates the movement of consciousness suggested by Bardon. Again Divine Life Society have the definitive free book on this entitled 'Nidra Yoga'. My view is that if you have difficulty, seek more information elsewhere. It is abundant.

SOFB: Now let us move onto the subject Ayahuasca as I know from some of your posts that this has been a part of your journey. Can you tell us how you came to get involved with it and how it impacted your path? From the little I know from your website it sounds like an amazing experience.

Scott: I have lived in Chile for 15 years. I heard about ayahuasca and was fascinated by the stories but was married with kids and didn't see myself getting to Peru. I had NO interest in magic or consciousness at the time. I was an atheist who never meditated and liked to drink beer . However, by chance, I discovered a shaman 3 miles from my house. I started doing ceremonies twice a month for a couple of years. The first message ayahuasca gave me was 'MAGIC EXISTS' . At the time that was mind blowing, but i hadn't seen anything yet. Of course ayahuasca is only 1 plant in an ecosystem of over 4000 medicinal amazonian plants many of them equal or more powerful than ayahuasca. MY shaman was also a sanangero, a specialist in the super powerful master plant chiric sanango and I participated in dietas of chiric sanango in conjunction with ayahuasca. This as well as many other plant dietas changed my life forever. Several times during ceremonies I had what could be described as kundalini experiences, including once when my shaman opened my chakras by singing icaros into them. After a couple of years I started to investigate 'what is magic?' because clearly it existed. One day I stumbled upon and read IIH. After i read it i went out into the garden and thought I would try moving my consciousness into a leaf to see what happened. I guess because my consciousness was already so wide open from all those ceremonies I made pretty much instant contact with an elemental. It kind of freaked me out . Later that week having dinner with my mother I accidentally evoked a demon. I was just sitting chatting and suddenly became aware of a horned female character identifying itself as Astarte. This was a terrifying experience and many others were to follow which I learned may have corresponded to what Robert Bruce calls 'chakra strobing' - basically having so much blocked energy in a chakra that when it is released trans dimensional communication is possible. This is classic imbalance of the elements.

Something had changed and this began maybe 2 years of uncontrolled spontaneous demonic evocations and other less frightening mystical experiences. This is what can happen without elemental balance. What seemed to happen is that when I focused my mind on anything I would instantly move through the depth point into other spiritual dimensions. After more study and consultations with other shamans I began a process of plant dietas which assisted the elemental balance a lot. I also did various kambo ceremonies and I think it was the 6th one where I had the energetic breakthrough. After that and a couple of years of deep meditation I achieved control over evocation so that it generally only happens intentionally through meditation. Ayahuasca is an extremely powerful substance which gets a lot of press but its the other plants which are really more the teacher plants. Plants like huaira caspi, ajos sacha, uchu sanango, bobinsana, punga amarilla, camalonga...the list goes on and on. Many of these plants specifically teach you how to use energy, how to remove entities, how to create healing recipes and how to do shamanic magic using song and symbols.

SOFB: The entities you experience through Ayahuasca and/or D.M.T how do you feel these relate to the view of reality we are given via IIH, PME and KTQ. Where would these entities fit into this picture?

Scott: I've thought a lot about this over the years. MY view is that KTQ and shamanic icaros are basically interfaces into the same power. KTQ focuses on sound and color and musical vibrational correspondences. So do shamanic icaros and these icaros and wisdom are usually in my experience only shared by the plant if you are occupying a space of pure consciousness. Well the healing knowledge is shared at that level. If your vibration is lower, you get other kinds of knowledge which are dangerous. For example how to enchant and seduce. I haven't done much work trying to integrate these. Each is already so staggeringly powerful. I confess though that there is something so incredibly beautiful about the shamanic path. It is not structured and organised like KTQ but the plants speak to us and guide us and often in beautiful symbols and lead us to new levels of consciousness. For example, one tree started showing me where the chakras exists in trees and how to connect with them. Eventually it is not necessary to take the plants. They speak to us still when we meditate and can guide us into full realization much as Bardon envisions his course of teaching will do.

Maybe someone will say these plant spirits are lowly vegetable kingdom spirits, but the ayahuma tree is also found in India and is present at all the temples of Shiva. I know im not the only person to have had an overwhelming Shiva experience taking this plant medicine.

Generally taking a tree we can sometimes meet the tree spirit itself but that golden pillar of light which is its spirit is often surrounded by protective spirits who test you to see if you deserve to be in this golden hallowed place. If you are lucky enough to advance and pass the tests the tree seems to become a kind of gateway and you can meet any spirit from any dimension you care to, although often the tree itself maintains a dominant voice in your mind. The voice is often strict and demanding, but the level of knowledge they have to impart is astounding...overwhelming...sometimes too much lol.

Ayahuasca ceremonies are known for their evocations of spirits. The shaman uses protective incense or tobacco smoke to seal a circle around the participants. The light is lowered. Invocations/Icaros are incanted. Of course unlike PME, the user might have less control over where exactly the journey will go. The discipline and control of magic is very attractive and I think Rawn Clark has pointed out that controlling consciousness through meditation leads to much greater perceivable depths. This is difficult for ayahuasca or dmt or mescaline users to believe, but there are similarities.

Its fascinating that Bardon pinpoints which elements are suppressed by which substances, Is he right? I'm not sure. My view of ayahuasca and the medicine ecosystem is that it is designed to balance the elements when used correctly. The plants specifically tell you exactly how to do it. It is not left to chance.

Sometimes I see the Ayahuasca ecosystem as the Key to the True Consciousness.

SOFB: Now you offer some courses on your website, could these be said to be the fruit of your experiences with Ayascha and Hermetics? Could you tell us more about these as they look perfect for beginning students of IIH.

Scott: Yes I would say that was true. Especially the first class Reprogram your Matrix which in some ways was based on IIH. As I moved further into meditation I was more and more pulled in the tantric direction and my last class Tactics of Tantra goes into that in some detail.

A lot of online offerings I've noticed offer exercises and some insight and are very good but with my course I really put a lot of effort into finding textual references to my own experiences. So if i say such and such a technique might be useful based on my experience , I usually back it up with reference to give it more context into whatever tradition might be relevant. I put quite a lot of effort into all of them and i'm not just gliding by on my accumulated knowledge.

SOFB: Mental Travel and Franz Bardons specific approach to Astral travel. How significant were these skills in your development. What I mean here is was your worldview impacted at all after completing these steps in what you experience upon being successful in the training?

Scott: They didn't have much of an impact until later. I found myself astral projecting spontaneously during the period before sleep. The first time it happened a spirit came to me and told me to repeat a mantra 3 times -' hail Mary, mother of grace, I'm ready to fly'. I did it and was projected out of the house. Through the roof. At one point I would just close my eyes and already be in another dimension. But these experiences were uncontrolled and tapered off as I gained energetic control. My guess this was due to kundalini awakening which i didn't really acknowledge until I received shaktipat earlier this year. Eventually, I actually ended up doing a similar technique to Bardon's. Imagine a copy of myself in a mirror then blow energy into it and I am out of body. But generally I don't formally try to astral project much. I just meditate and i find myself meeting spirits pretty fast. Often dead people and the like wander into awareness but I tend to avoid them and move to higher vibrations using the elements as a guide to where I am at vibrationally.

SOFB: How important is it to do the Astral Travel training of Step 9 in the way Franz Bardon explains rather then creating some sort of Astral double or illusory body without the Mental/Astal separation before integration? As much of what is read about all seems to point to practitioners taking the later approach and not the former challenging approach of Bardon.

Scott: Bardon is the expert on this clearly. I haven't thought about it so much and dont have the granularity of awareness that he had. No shame in admitting that. I tend to work intuitively with the information that comes to guide me.

SOFB: PME and KTQ. What have these books brought to your practice? We know these are very private but would appreciate anything you can share.

Scott: I've kind of avoided PME just because I can't be bothered with all the ceremony and because I can evoke pretty much any spirit I want through meditation. However, its true sometimes i work ceremonially using just the imagination which is something I think Bardon mentions and certainly Wlliam Gray mentions this in his VERY excellent books.

While I might draw a circle of light imaginatively, I am way more interested in feeling what I call the viscosity of consciousness, which is becoming super aware of the elemental qualities as we alchemize thoughts from earth through to akasha. When done successfully the metaphor of a lotus allows one to be conscious of all these planes simultaneously. It has a quality of such perfectly beautiful transparency which is beyond imagination while exhibiting these subtle changes in 'viscosity'. At that level infusing the elements with the qualities of God is about the most wonderful experience to be had.

This of course ties into KTQ which is basically completely based on infusing consciousness with the qualities of God. I've done quite a bit of it but to be honest have found myself out of my depth a few times and had to pull back very carefully. You might think you can handle invoking the first 5-10 letters but infusing your consciousness with this much infinity can be dangerous. You have to move slowly as Bardon advises.

As a side note on dangers, William Gray has an exercise which involves using the elemental shapes of the tarot - swords, wands, cups, pentacles - as metaphors for thought and then working on infusing each thought with these metaphors and then maybe changing the form of them, for example making the swords (thoughts) larger. It's another form of infusing consciousness with divinity. However, you MUST be elementally balanced. I didn't even try this exercise out formally but as i read it my mind just started ruminating out of curiosity. If you've ever seen mickey mouse in the sorcerer's apprentice, this is what started happening in my mind. Basically an infinite loop was created where all my thoughts were extending out into infinity and without the comfort of knowing 'the trip will be over soon'. Some information in some books can lead to madness if you are not prepared. Luckily I had countermeasures available and lived to warn other curious souls. I was lucky. This was way more scary than any demon I have ever met. Be very careful and honest about what you are really capable of.

SOFB: Did the way you saw IIH change after moving onto these books? In that it was preparing you for something?

Scott: Sure, but there's a transition period where you wonder 'how much power do I actually need' or 'omg i really am in God's workshop'. Transitioning the mind to the reality of infinite creative possibilities can be overwhelming. This is not a game. Karma is real. Tread with great care and with the right intention to do good.

SOFB: Lastly is there anything else you would like to add that you feel is important for students of IIH.

Scott: No one talks about this but I think its an important topic. Sexuality is skipped in most books but it is where, for many people, imbalances are rife. I advocate occasionally using sexuality as the object of meditation. THere are a couple of reasons for this. Firstly sexuality is by its nature fire and most people have no issues allowing their mind to ruminate over sexual content. People tell me 'I can't visualize a ball of energy' but they have no issues visualizing a bikini model for extended periods of time. It's a matter of becoming more conscious. This makes extended meditation and the generation and accumulation of energy very easy and a lot of fun. There is alot of talk in new age circles of tantric sex or energy orgasms. I have experienced this but in my view this should be a non physical non masturbatory approach. It is a contemplation of and complete acceptance of the shadow.

Of course people like Lon Milo Duquette point to different interpretations of sexual energy for example in his book on Sex Magic, Tantra and Tarot he encourages ritualistic sex to exhaustion while focusing on tarot images and the sharing of sexual fluids. Crowley also has some amazing meditations in the Libers which are worth checking out in this vein. I'm not sure any of this is necessary. I wonder about the implications, but im sure its fun.

Its common to say that tantra is not about sex, but if you actually read the tantras you will find plenty of sexual content. Sexuality is the primary manifestation of divinity within us and we throw shade upon it and avoid it. This lower octave of divinity provides a direct passage into higher consciousness when it is treated as such.

This does have its dangers too and its possible to become obsessive and not release the sexual object and move to higher vibrations. Dangers include direct confrontation with demonic and vampiric energies. This doesn't happen so often, but it's worth mentioning as extreme countermeasures are sometimes necessary. These kinds of spirits are extremely dangerous and can totally corrupt and take over your thought stream. Go wisely.

SOFB: Thank you for sharing so much with us.

BOB

Introduction to Bob

Bob has led a pretty full life as you will see from his interviews, as a result of this life of searching, discovering and practice he founded 'Sixty Skills' so this is perhaps the best way to introduce Bob, by introducing Sixty Skills:

> Sixty Skills is transforming the traditional transmission of meditative, and yogic, instruction from one of master to disciple to a modern online learning format. Sixty Skills has covered the globe and over a thirty year period derived the key techniques from all the major schools of Buddhism, Hermetics, Hindu-Yogic, and Taoist practice.

Interview

SOFB: Firstly could I ask you to introduce yourself to the readers, please tell us a little about yourself and how you first discovered Franz Bardon's books.

Bob: I made the usual rounds of traditional Chinese martial arts (specifically Yang style Tai cChi and Clyman's nei gung from Temple Style, Bagua, and Hsing Yi), took in a few Buddhist empowerments over the years (most notably the Emei Mountain Sudden Enlightenment School, Pure Land, the Medicine Buddha, etc.) and studied with a Taoist practitioner, but none of it really stuck. I was good at it and didn't really care. I even tried the Golden Dawn material for awhile. It wasn't until I ran into Bardon's material that things clicked.

As for Bardon's material I ran into Mark Rasmus at a seminar, I thought he was sincere and I went to visit him in Thailand. Over the next three years I worked through the first and third book. The second book is not a big focus of mine, although I have been working more with the planets lately.

SOFB: In every interview I like to ask some standard questions about sticking points found in IIH:

VOM: Franz Bardon said he expected step 1 to be completed inside of 2 weeks. Do you think this was realistic or the first of many tests of the students 'Will'.

Bob: The real issue with this is that learning any of the material in the book from another person is much easier than learning it from a book. Perhaps it has something to do with learning via transmission, but in general it shouldn't take more than an afternoon to learn how to perform the techniques involved. It can take up to a month to be able to perform the initial focusing exercises for approximately 5 minutes, which seems to be the "magic" point where it becomes useful. More is better in general, however anything over 20 minutes doesn't seem to make much of a difference.

VISUALIZATION: People tend to spend years here expecting IMAX like results, what is your advice for those on these Step 2 exercises. Did you follow the method from IIH or come up with your own approach?

Bob: The auto-suggestion exercises are fantastic for changing bad habits. I've taught these to a variety of people and everyone reports good results. It's also a technique anyone can use. The key thing is to make sure you use a positive command. It must be something you want to do. Choose one thing to work on and run a string of beads directly upon waking and directly before going to sleep. The whole process should take about ten minutes. Do this for 30 days straight. For a really ingrained habit it might take 100 days. Don't stress when you fail in the beginning. Just let it go and keep practicing. Over time this will happen less and less often. Then you won't think about it anymore and it becomes a natural behavior.

I found the sensory gate exercises to be fairly straight forward. Perhaps this is because my sense of smell is the most developed of my senses and having an earth correspondence it makes everything else easier. I don't really have any advice for this. But I had already spent years working on a five element Taoist system and running the orbits from both Clyman and Morris' material. Visualizing light, the sensation of energy, etc were all old hat.

The pore breathing and posture exercises are two critical components of the first book.

Pore breathing is critical as this is how you will engage with all of the other energies (elemental, astral, mental, Akasha and even non-dual light) until such a time as you can open the energy center above your head and stream it directly down into the body.

You do not "visualize" fire energy so much as you breathe it in to the body while sensing its heat, seeing its red color, and hearing its Sch sound as an example. As another example, when you breath astral energy in time slows, you feel that soft sensation and some people even hear sounds like chimes. But you are still breathing it into and out of the pores into the center of the body and out again via the hands/pores/orifices/etc.

A key component to always perform is to program what you want the energy to be BEFORE you begin pore breathing. This is especially important with vital energy. And is even more important when it comes to the letters of the third book. Otherwise, the energy defaults to your background belief settings and tends to make those stronger. So sick people stay sick, weak people stay weak, manic people stay manic, etc. Spend a moment making the energy what you want it to be. Some schools refer to this as the secret smile technique. It is important and mostly speed bumped in the text.

The key to being a magician is in bending reality to your will. This includes yourself.

The asana exercise is Bardon's only contribution to training the structure of the body in his book. This is a very lengthy subject and not well presented in a written format. The posture holding exercises of the Taoist internal martial arts are typical of these. These can be performed via movement and frequently use resistance as well. They can build and/or integrate the soft tissue of the body depending upon what is done. The short answer is the better you can stack your structure the more efficiently your body will move energy.

VITAL FORCE: Some people cannot feel the accumulation, what can they do to feel it more intensively?

Bob: Rasmus has an exercise called building the ball. In this you pore breath vital energy in and exhale from the palms forming a ball between the hands. You then play with the ball.

What a student is looking to do is to feel the boundary layer of the ball between their hands. Rasmus has a very good video on Vimeo on how to do this. I highly recommend this. Most of the better systems out there have an exercise like this. I learned it originally years ago from a Taoist system. It can take up to ten hours of practice to do this, but most people can do it much quicker. I've rarely seen it take more than a week of consistent practice to master.

SOFB: Also seeing that you are a person who likes to use weights for your physical health, have you found ways to integrate the two?

Bob: Aside from Jesus allergy and a strange predilection for weird diets, the next biggest obstacle to achievement in this work for most practitioners is the pathological aversion to the concept that being physically strong makes your energy strong.

Anyone who has spent time around physically strong people quickly realizes they have strong energy as well. The quickest way to become physically strong is to use barbells. Martin Faulks demonstrating a 200kg deadlift is a good example. It is also the quickest way to develop strong energy. Most of the astral exercises are about learning to manipulate energy, but in and of themselves do little to increase strength at it.

Additionally, the basic barbell movements also build the tendon network in the body very effectively. And the stronger that is, the stronger energy moves in the body. It's not complicated.

So, I use weightlifting to build tissue and maintain strength. The tendon training exercises teach you how to manipulate the electric, and magnetic, currents and further integrate the tissue.

Being fat on the other hand slows energy down. So, an ideal magician would be both strong and lean. Without steroids, most people will put on fat with muscle. You then diet the fat off. You can become very strong this way. Lama Gant, for example, could deadlift 525pounds/238kg at a bodyweight of 123pounds/56kg.

On a practical basis, if you can squat 1.5 times your bodyweight and deadlift twice your bodyweight you are good to go. Additionally, once you've gotten to this point, you don't need to maintain the muscle mass required to do it for life. The ligaments/tendons stick around long after you lose the muscle due to inactivity/age. As does the strength of your energy.

Keep in mind that the bodyweight you gain doing this is directly related to your caloric intake. If you eat a lot you get bigger and stronger faster. If you don't, it takes longer but you are smaller. The lightweight lifers in powerlifting and Olympic weightlifting are superhumanly strong. If you ever meet some of these people, you will find their energy is also amazingly strong as well.

While a lot of classical systems didn't have access to barbells, almost all of them held objects while in posture, used heavy weighted weapons, wore weighted vests, etc. They were simply using resistance to increase their ability to generate and move energy.

On a basic level your ability to focus and the size/integration of your ligaments and tendons determines how strong your energy is. If you want to be really strong at the physical generation of energy, you need both.

This gets confusing as most magicians are lazy and weak willed. As a result, they use spirit infused magic to have an entity throw the appropriate switches within their body allowing them to run more of something than they can on their own. Aside from being very physically destructive over time this also results in a very fucked up kind of dependence upon the entity. It also explains a lot of the questionable decision making in this community as well. Maintain your sovereignty. None of these things are giving you anything you can't do on your own. And none of them are doing it for free. Franz Bardon himself was an excellent cautionary tale in this regard.

ELEMENTS: Getting in contact with what Rawn Clark called the principle of the element can be difficult as at that point the student has no real idea of what this is. When it is make believe and when this goal is finally achieved. What are your thoughts here?

Bob: Here is a fundamental problem that has no good solution.

The easiest way to get around this is to practice the elements from day one as Kabbalah using three point focus (sound, sensation and color). The problem with this is that without being initiated into this, or having prior experience, the letters are incredibly harsh. I've had people without these things go directly into the elements as Kabbalah and describe scenarios where working with water as the letter M initially felt like someone stabbing them in the liver with a freezing dagger. It takes a lot of balls to keep going under circumstances like that.

Bardon's books are in the order they are so someone can do it without a teacher. In this regard, doing the planets first gives you a good preparation and many potential internal guides to walk you through the letters.

Without this, just going through the elements is very slow. The only advice I can give is to pay attention to the sensation as much as possible. Make sure your pore breathing and posture are well developed. Understand that you train the physical component via a strongly audible vocalization with the tendons engaged and your attention focused on the lower abdomen. Astral is a whisper with the tendons engaged and your attention focused on the solar plexus. Mental is silent with a focus on the center of the head.

DEPTH POINT: This is perhaps a big development in IIH where a big shift has to occur in order to understand the point Franz Bardon was trying to make. Can you comment on the significance of this exercise?

Bob: Very important. The depth point is crucial as this is how an earth body type conducts out of body projection. People who are very grounded generally cannot do this from the head until they master the depth point exercise using the solar plexus.

The easiest way to do this is to imagine you are shrinking and collapsing down into your solar plexus. Down, down, down. Faster and faster. Until you are screaming downward. Jumping out of an airplane in freefall is slow in comparison. At the end of it I usually crash land on what appears to be a small hill. Around the base of this are all of my prior incarnations. In front of me is a flat wall carved into the side of a cave. I generate a huge screen of Akasha at the front of the wall. Then I fly into the Akasha.

At this point I am in the Akasha and project to wherever I am going to. I go deeper and deeper into the Akasha. I go until all of my senses are blocked out. Then and only then when I am completely wreathed in Akasha, I call on the letter, planets, wherever of where I want to go. At first this will appear as a flickering light. It gets stronger and stronger as I key into the vibratory, or energetic, state of the thing. Then I slam into it.

Keep in mind this takes you to the astral level representation of a thing.

Projecting out of the head is more a matter of separating my mental body from my astral-mental matrix and floating off to where I want to go. The rope suspension method works well here.

SOFB: Can you comment on the difference between the spatial center of a thing and the depth point of a thing.

The spatial center is just that. The middle of something. You perceive the world from its viewpoint. I learned how to do this with a clay Buddhist medallion. You can also get some background information on its construction. Animals I haven't worked with much. Human beings you can ride like a meat suit when you get good at this, but this is a severe violation of their freewill and not advisable. Also, their energy, emotions and memories backflow into you as well. And most people are a filthy mess. As one of my teachers once said, "it is what we do not know about others that allows us to work with them." Caveat emptor.

The depth point is an altered state of experiencing something generally at the astral level. Here trees have consciousness, the laws of physics bend and shit starts to get weird. Depending upon where you interact things can be very similar to the here and now or much less so. You can also branch off into the mental and Akashic levels of something quickly as well. Maintaining your focus here is important.

GESTURE: Not much is ever heard about the application of Gesture training to create our own finger rituals. Has this been a useful part of your training and if so how have you applied these rituals in your training and daily life.

Bob: Very important. Anything you need to be able to do quickly and on the fly is best conducted with this. You can also link this to sigil magic as well, but I'm not going to get into that here as that is a rather involved process.

The easiest way to do this is to project into the Akasha. While there complete a ritual to do whatever it is you would normally do that you want associated with the gesture. Make the gesture. Do this a couple of times. Use one gesture for turning it on and one gesture to turn it off. Leave the Akasha. Then practice whatever it is you programed the gesture to do without all of the intermediate steps.

I have one gesture on call for Fajin (A term used in Tai Chi and Internal Arts for expressing explosive force). That way I can do this whenever I need to without lining up, getting ready, etc. This is a pretty common application in the Chinese martial arts community where these old codgers use a gesture they generated 30 years ago to Fajin with. Its why they never get any better and you can't figure out how they are doing it. It's also why they are essentially stealing from their students and are assholes in general. If the guy isn't willing to break things down into component steps and teach you how to do it tell him to fuck off and spend your money elsewhere.

I've got another for single pointed focus. Since I tend to get a little ADD at times it allows me to get more done.

Keep in mind potential "gestures" cover a lot of ground. And not all of these require a physical movement that is visible using the hands.

The downside to gestures is also worth talking about. If you use a gesture to do something you don't get better at it by just using the gesture. In essence whatever level of ability you had going into the Akasha to generate it is where you are stuck. To get better at something, you still need to practice all of your component parts in sequence. Then you go back into the Akasha and upgrade the gesture again.

Also, other people with enough sensitivity can copy your gestures and use them. So, keep this to yourself.

SOFB: Though of course working through IIH has to have had an enormous impact upon who you are, did this have any overt impact upon on your working and public life and how others saw you?

Bob: In general, these kinds of practices make you more of whatever you are. If you are a good person underneath it all things tend to work out. If you have any personality defects, it tends to amplify that. All that said, misbehavior is an issue particularly when you start to come into your own power. Everyone does it. Good people get over it. I still cringe thinking about some of the things that happened.

It made the latter part of my military career possible. I deployed for the last time in my mid-forties. Now, I wasn't the fastest guy out there, but I could still pull my own weight. Without these practices it simply wouldn't have happened.

Shortly after I went through kundalini awakening it caused a lot of problems. I was young and my physical energy was very strong. This polarized the reaction of other people toward me. Part of the problem is that the Chinese systems I trained in only taught me what amounts to the electric pathway in Hermetics. After learning how to manipulate the magnetic force a lot of problems, including personality related, resolved themselves.

All of this greatly complicated my relationship with people of power (general officers, politicians, high level civilian officials, etc.). At the end of the day, they know at some level you are not their servant. And ultimately, they do not like this at all. This is not a negative thing either. Powerful people don't spend lots of time with peers. They are surrounded by people helping them achieve their goals. And if you are not doing that, your being there is a distraction. If they view you as a threat, it's much worse. To this day I can't get into most night clubs by myself as I tend to set the bouncers off.

When you generate a certain amount of physical/astral/mental energy it tends to set people off a little even subconsciously, but they can deal with that. Once you begin to generate Akasha and non-dual light, unless people are family members or very close friends they generally start to avoid you. I've lost a lot of friends this way. It pretty much screws you out of any long term employment working for others. At the end, you have to work for yourself.

Part of this is that the energy you produce changes people when they are around you. Akasha in general represents the chaotic power of the void. That primordial chaos out of which duality sprang. People who have this are quite literally capable of anything. They can bypass most egregores at will. And most people really aren't into this. And this is assuming you aren't doing this intentionally. If you are, you are an asshole. But if you aren't, you are weirding them out and they don't like it. Most people get divorced when going through this as well.

And, if the practitioner is male and straight, their wife usually goes through some kind of energetic development as well. Women generally absorb large amounts of energy when an empowered man has sex with them. In this regard, women can achieve development just by regularly having sex with a powerfully developed man.

Also, people who spend large amounts of time around you gradually get exposed to otherworldly things. And when it happens often enough, they can't cognitively dissonance their way out of it. At that point they become afraid of you. And that sucks. It sucks really hard. I still speak with one of my best friends I had as a young man almost monthly. I haven't been to his new house in the three years he moved.

SOFB: We asked earlier about sticking points that some have trouble with but in your rise through IIH did you also come across steps that caused you real trouble? If so, how did you get past this and move on?

Bob: Not really. The main thing is that a lot of these skills take an extended period of practice to master. The clairvoyance based skills can take years by themselves depending upon personal constitution. Which is why once you learn how to practice a given skill you move on to the next chapter while continuing to practice that skill. The whole thing of not moving on until you master something is a formula for failure if you are working by yourself. Also, the book is remarkably mis-organized.

The more I find out about Bardon himself points in the direction of his being mostly a ritual/evocation style practitioner who wrote an internal power book. And that makes sense. Every picture I've seen of the guy makes him look like a sack of potatoes. And the chain smoking would have limited internal power after a certain point anyway. My guess is that he wrote the book while under the influence of a spirit entity via mediumship/channeling.

Even a lot of his Kabbalah points in the direction of mental with some astral level effects. Which you can pull off without much body training assuming a spirit entity is throwing the switches. It's not like he was using this to physically manifest fire or to run 100km at a time.

SOFB: We have had some questions from the community in regard to the energetic model in IIH compared to methods shown for example in Yogic systems or Taoist Cultivation systems. So we see in both Yogic and Taoist methods a refining of the energy and a slow rise either through central channel and chakras or from dantien, mid and upper via the microcosmic orbit. Do you have any experience of these other systems and how those methods compare energetically (for example Kundalini) to what is occurring in IIH.

Bob: That's a good question.

On a fundamental level one of the big takeaways from going through Kundalini is the ability to generate Akasha. I'm not sure you can generate, or harness, Akasha without it.

If you look at icons of certain Buddhist saints, Fudo Myo is popular, you will see a thin band of purple in the energetic field around the saint. That's Akasha. The problem is that none of the Asian systems bother to explain what that means and how to use it. Which creates a lot of problems as you have any number of people walking around with the ability to fundamentally warp reality and no real control over it. It also turns most people into spirit magnets and this results in their being manipulated a lot. These people can be remarkably unstable.

A couple of ways exist to go through the Kundalini. You can condense and circulate vital force via the orbits until it explodes up the central channel/spine, you can keep slamming vital force up against your crown until it breaks open (mostly yogic), a teacher can open it via transmission (i.e. Shaktipat) or you can frequently establish equilibrium using a four element system (i.e. Bardon).

But because of this, most of these systems do not result in your ability to manipulate the elements with any strength as they are working with vital force and Akasha predominantly. Fine for enlightenment. Crappy for working magic.

The first three tend to happen fairly quickly and often explosively. Using equilibrium on the other hand is a fairly slow process whereby you keep practicing and then one day you notice this weird purple stuff creeping into your elemental work.

Kundalini awakening started in my case at the age of 13. I was from a not particularly religious family in south Texas. It took another decade to figure out what was going on. I met my Taoist teacher in my late 20's, read Glenn Morris' books and I was off to the races.

The main issue is that the equilibrium method lacks a certain density to the development of physical energy that the orbits do provide. It comes with many fewer side effects than the traditional yogic methods tend to come with. I also think it is much better for longevity and health over the long term. The yogic method of up and out is depleting over the long term in my experience. People become emaciated. And the orbits tend to damage the metabolism/thyroid over time as well from what I've seen. Guys get fat.

In all, the equilibrium method is one of the main contributions of Bardon's work to esoteric development.

SOFB: Mental Travel and Franz Bardons specific approach to Astral travel. How significant were these skills in your development. What I mean here is was your worldview impacted at all after completing these steps in what you experience upon being successful in the training?

Bob: Pretty important. Due to being very physically grounded projection out of the head using the mental body was something that took way too much effort and rarely happened. Until I learned Bardon's system. For people in this position you must learn to project via the depth point exercise at the solar plexus before you will develop any real ability to mentally project at will. Perhaps this has something to do with elevating the energy in the body via the energy centers. I really don't know. I have seen this progression solve the problem for people who had spent years trying to project from the head with no success. And keep in mind I had already been through the Kundalini using the orbits and still couldn't project from the head for the most part.

As for my worldview, it didn't change that much. I'd already been through the Kundalini and experienced immersion into non-dual light. What it did was give me a much greater ability to explore the Kabbalistic realms and to engage the denizens of the other layers of reality on my terms versus theirs. It was basically the difference between always playing defense and going on the offensive. Or for those who have issues with that language it's the difference between being a passive participant and an active one.

Evocation takes an outsized level of importance in Western magical practice for the same reason. Since many people lack the internal development, or natural ability, to travel to these places they bring that world to them instead. It is the primary strength of the ritual systems.

SOFB: How important is it to do the Astral Travel training of Step 9 in the way Franz Bardon explains rather then creating some sort of Astral double or illusory body without the Mental/Astral separation before integration? As much of what is read about all seems to point to practitioners taking the later approach and not the former challenging approach of Bardon.

Bob: The fact that this is left out of the book despite the many fantasy elements the translator injection to what Bardon originally wrote is completely baffling to me. And to people who have not gotten to this point write this down.

Being able to separate your astral body allows you to control the time of your death.

If you can only travel via the mental body, when it comes time to die, you will suffer just the same way everyone else does. And that is the real value of having control over your astral body as a separate entity. If you gained nothing else from all of your training, that by itself would make all of the work worth it.

The training is very uncomfortable and potentially dangerous. The warnings to be in a locked room by yourself without an open window that a fly can come in through are crucial. You can die practicing this. You are going to die at some point without it. Best to gain control of this process in advance.

SOFB: PME and KTQ. What have these books brought to your practice? We know these are very private but would appreciate anything you can share.

Bob: I'm much more of a Kabbalist than an evoker. In fact, I worked my way through KTQ before I did anything with PME. My main work with PME centered around developing resistance to the influence of the entities contained therein.

KTQ is much more useful on a tactical level as it is done via an internal power model and can be engaged on the fly without a big ritual buildup. It is also free of the influence of the entities in the third book. Applying it strategically is much more difficult as an entity is not there to do the work for you. You have to fully form the volts being put together and fully direct it. With PME the entity is working for you 24/7 for as long as they are tasked. Ultimately you are the power source either way, but in one you are on your own and the other you get worked over.

Some things for readers to consider. A true demonic entity will shrug off Akasha by itself as they are largely associated with Saturn. However, the E-N letter combination can be weaponized to energetically sterilize a space and get rid of these creatures. Likewise, the E-U combination can be used as well under the right situations.

Breaking with an entity whose school you have formally joined, as in one of the 360 Earth Heads, is very uncomfortable. It can be done, but you basically have to destroy everything you built with them (ritual implements, books written, et al) and formally release them. Then you run large amounts of Akasha through the energy center above the head for a few months. It will also be physically painful at times.

The E-N letter combination can be used to chase them off for awhile as the connection fades. Performing the compound moves in weightlifting while generating the E-N letter combination greater increases your power to use the combination. The reason for this is that once you make a pact with them, they bond with the energy center above your head and then control your access to Akasha and non-dual light. And yes, that is just as bad an idea as that sounds. It is much better to pay them off with ritual offerings with a clear understanding that the good stuff is not on the table.

As far as the letters are concerned, keep in mind that it is very important to program what you are looking for with the characteristics of the letter (Akashic, mental, astral and physical) before you start to work with them. It takes at least 10 hours of continual practice with a since letter to be able to generate that energy in a stable manner. Also, you need to be clear as to what level of reality you are engaging the letter as this radically changes what you encounter.

SOFB: Did the way you saw IIH change after moving onto these books? In that it was preparing you for something?

Bob: A lot of the exercises made much more sense. For example, the automatic writing stuff. FYI, that is how you get the seal for entities you encounter. Everything in there has a reason for being there. It may just be the case that you don't need it depending upon what you are doing.

Also, all of the exercises are building blocks that reinforce one another. So, it is okay to skip ahead as long as you keep practicing the earlier exercises to the point of mastery. And you'll want to revisit things you've previously mastered from time to time to amp up their performance.

SOFB: Lastly is there anything else you would like to add that you feel is important for students of IIH.

Bob: If you are interested in learning more about evocation and its central role in Western magic traditionally speaking check out the Glitch Bottle podcast. But always keep in mind you don't get anything for free and these things all have a price.

Always vet and evaluate carefully anything you learn from the great beyond.

Make the gods envy you.

View your life as a multi-episode cinematic movie extravaganza. And every time you are watching Netflix ask yourself, "Would someone want to watch me doing this or find this interesting?"

Then get to work.

SOFB: Thank you once again Bob.

BOB (INTERVIEW 2)

Introduction to Bob

Bob has led a pretty full life as you will see from his interviews, as a result of this life of searching, discovering and practice he founded 'Sixty Skills' so this is perhaps the best way to introduce Bob, by introducing Sixty Skills:

Sixty Skills is transforming the traditional transmission of meditative, and yogic, instruction from one of master to disciple to a modern online learning format. Sixty Skills has covered the globe and over a thirty year period derived the key techniques from all the major schools of Buddhism, Hermetics, Hindu-Yogic, and Taoist practice.

SOFB Community Questions

SOFB Community: First, if possible, what correlation between power and connective tissue; he said stronger connective tissue and tendons work makes for more wielding more power, I'd be interested to understand why from a hermetic point of view.

Bob: If you want to do something in the material world, you need a material point of transmission. Long before people can set things on fire with their mind, the conversion of astral phenomena to the physical most often happens via spontaneous discharge of astral energy into kinetic force. That force runs via the ligaments and tendons.

SOFB Community: Second, I'd like him to develop further on the topic of the earth zone and elemental spirits. From his writing, I understood that they have agendas and evil intents of using the initiate and controlling his access to akasha. From Bill and Virgil's writings however, they are benevolent spirits who are more than happy to offer knowledge and training for one asking for it and are offering guidance. It might be a misunderstanding I got from Bob's text but I'd like to know why does he discourage one from working with them.

Bob: I don't discourage people from learning from them. Just understand that nothing comes for free. These things work with people as a way of expressing themselves in the material world. If you are looking for guidance, they will manipulate your senses to push you in that direction. It's called getting what you asked for. The fact that any pact you make with them might very well last beyond the scope of your current lifetime is another often left out fact. For example, becoming a priest in an apostolic order gets you access to the use of the Latin Mass as a source of power. And that is profound. The Latin Mass is a 1600 year old battery that has been continually added to by millions of people every day for almost two millennia. Being anointed a priest marks you and seems to last more than one lifetime. But it is the pass key to the egregore that surrounds the Latin Mass and without it you cannot leverage it. You pay your money and make your choices.

Regarding the Akasha debate keep in mind that the advantage of undergoing internal power development is that you generate your own Akasha and non-dual light. If you have not done this work, a spirit entity providing it to you is a way around this limitation. But just like borrowing your father's car, he sets the ground rules for what you get to do with it.

SOFB Community: It is common for some folk traditions to have practices surrounding the concept of 'journeying' in order to engage with spirits. Here I refer to those using drums or alike as trance induction methods, not entheogens. How would you relate those in regards to mental wondering as a way to engage with spirits as provided by Bardon? And why do you feel that engaging with spirits is not as much as a taboo for those traditions in comparison to those following Bardon system.

Bob: The drums, and trance induction, are just another way to induce mental wandering. Nothing wrong with it at all. Drums as a practical matter seem to hone in on lower vibration spirits. Chimes, and bells, higher order.

If you are using mental wandering to engage spirits as in the second book, you are working with spirits. No taboo in Bardon's system exists. I just think that the issue of the bill being do for having the entity flip switches for you gets undersold.

SOFB Community: From the different methods to engage with spirits provided by Bardon (e.g., mental wondering, evocation), which one you had most success with? And which one would you see as the most achievable for students coming into PME?

Bob: I've done evocation and mental wandering predominantly. I'm beginning to work more with the crystal method as it seems to better establish dominance early on with less physical risk or energetic demand as required by physical evocation. Mental wandering requires the most development of the subtle senses. Your clairvoyance and clairaudience better be on point or you are going to get a lot of fantasy based garbage coming through. Evocation takes the most setup and energy. It can also be the most dangerous, but it requires little in the way of development of the subtle senses. They crystal method is in-between. Personally, if I had to do it all over again, I would have started with the crystal method. FYI, spirits hate this. To the degree they can feel pain, the crystal method hurts them. But it also greatly reduces their ability to mislead or lie. All three can work depending upon what you are working on.

However, if you want to learn a physical skill, mediumship is what you need to engage in. And it is the most physically draining of them all.

SOFB Community: The process of making consecrated tools is always a hot topic in grimoire based traditions. Some claim that every step should be followed by the letter while others are flexible to the point of skipping most of the tools. What's your approach in regards to the preparation and consecration of magical tools when working with PME?

Bob: If you are going to practice a system, you need to follow the rules until you know enough to break the rules. As a practical matter, the tools act as charged foci to engage spirits with. They don't see very well, but their sense of hearing and smell is very acute. So, while a paper crown painted gold with Hebrew script works well instilling your authority as a king, you still need to bath thoroughly, or the spirits won't come when conducting physical evocation. Likewise, a polyester faux lionskin belt cannot hold the charge the real thing does.

If you want to do mental wandering as your primary method, then get off your ass make sure your clairvoyance and clairaudience are on point. Your Akasha should be good as well to send the little bastards packing when the time comes.

If you want to be a ritual guy, then get all of your tools in order.

At a certain point, you can freestyle. But you have to be competent first or it is all a mess.

SOFB Community: Is it only the Earthzone ones that control access to akasha and non-dual light, or of other spheres as well? Why do you think that happens, does it have to do with they trying to keep you 'positively engaged' in incarnation and exploring the physical world, expanding universe etc, and not 'escaping' it, by achieving non-returner, or arahant, via non-dual light ?

Bob: I don't know. All I know is that if you enter into a relationship with anyone, you need to have certain things in common and that will track you in a certain direction.

Avoiding spirits and pursing the enlightenment path by itself has merit. But then again you probably won't be doing much magic either.

SOFB Community: (Read a Justin B post some time ago, said some of Earthzone Spirits seem like former magicians, some like egregores, and others like made-up energy currents or such) How does a being get to become such a spheric being as in PME, of any of the spheres, up to to Pluto ? Did they too have to incarnate and train hard into the physical world to achieve such godlike powers and be appointed such divine roles (not referring to the inhabitants of those spheres)?

Bob: I can give one example. The Black School of Saint Cyprian is internally run by a former magician turned saint. Then end goal of the system is enrollment in the Order of Melchizedek and the transformation of human magicians into angels of the Lord. For example, according to that system, Metatron was a human magician named Enoch.

SOFB Community: The Kabalistic letters, the primary energies and the planetary energies run via specific bands of connective tissue within the body"

Rawn: http://abardoncompanion.de/KTQ-Steps1-5.html :

"In Hebrew kabbalistic practice, there are not only notes associated with each letter (by way of the vowel points) but also a specific movement that accompanies each vowel's pronunciation"

How are those postures/movements discovered and cultivated, so as to help condense the planetary energies, and Letters as dense as possible into the physical? Does the Letter practice guide one intuitively? I'm assuming concentration plays a major part as well, besides the physical posture/anchor of sorts?

Bob: Three pointed focus forms the base: color, sound and sensation. By training the tendons/ligaments it results in a kind of clairsentience that as you vibrate the sound through the ligaments/tendons results in the body spontaneously forming certain postures/hand gestures/movements. These will be largely individualized to the practitioner and therefore free of a lot of the baggage associated with the egregores around something like a traditional mudra/body posture.

Only do this with Kabbalah. Traditionally the aspect of a planet is divided into the: various intelligences of a planet and the spirit of the planet. Bardon's second book is a listing of planetary intelligences. They are useful for information. Each planet has only one planetary spirit and this represents its raw power. The planetary spirits (not intelligences as presented in Bardon's second book) have an aspect in the physical world that can literally rip you apart. Accidentally slipping into the planetary spirit aspect at various points in time has caused me a seizure, burned my nervous system and other rather unpleasant side effects. This only occurred as I've done a lot of tendon training over they years. Most people without this training won't get anything except astral and mental level side effects from trying to work with the spirit of a planet within their own body as it has no ability to ground into the physical.

SOFB Community: Kether and non-dual light relation, differences etc?

Bob: As far as I view it they are the same. Non-dual light is something that can only be defined in the negative (i.e. by that which it is not).

SOFB Community: What are the requirements to "engage the denizens of the other layers of reality on my terms versus theirs," specifically in the context of QBL (Qabalah) and the Godhead? Does "on my terms" imply receiving information or assistance without any form of pact, formal or informal, as long as one meets the necessary requirements and the denizens willingly help others in recognition of their Divine authority?

Bob: Nothing comes for free. Ever. By being in the power position, you at least have a better chance of setting the terms. Again, you pay your money and take your chances.

SOFB Community: If one cultivates non-dual light, and achieves non-returner, what's the purpose of IIH Step 10, 4 fundamental qualities of Godhead? Only to provide godlike authority for PME practice with the spirits of the spheres, or other?

Bob: The godhead exercises strike me as the Western equivalent of the deity fusion practices out of Asia.

SOFB Community: Does the practice of Step 10 in Franz Bardon's "Initiation into Hermetics" (IIH), which involves cultivating four qualities of the Godhead, have the potential to build a supernatural and godlike Ego or authority? Are there any potential dangers or traps associated with this process?

Bob: It's deity fusion. You act more like whatever deity you are bonding with.

SOFB Community: How can the practices of Trekcho, Thogal, and the attainment of Rainbow body be approached from a Hermetic perspective?

Bob: I suspect, but do not know, that the rainbow body practices have something to do with the letters I and J. As they both generate rainbow like colors in the aura. If you are talking trulkhor that is another issue entirely. The letter I in particular greases the movement between the physical and astral powerfully. The letter J has a lot to do with the "meta" sensation tantric Buddhism strives to generate. Beyond that anything I have to say is a guess.

SOFB Community: I have a simple question for Bob. Does he use Soul Mirrors (Black and White) in his practice, and how does he work on bringing the Elements into equilibrium?

Bob: I don't ever use soul mirrors. I establish equilibrium by placing the elements into the four sections of the body repeatedly throughout the day (fire in the head, air in the upper chest, water in the abdomen and earth in the legs).

SOFB Community: Would you say that the actual perception and recognition of the nature of the spirits of the spheres and EZ differs for the practitioner who has gone through KTQ before PME? How would you characterize that difference if there is one?

Bob: Hard to say. It was the way I did it. I suspect so, but I lack enough data points to give you a definite answer. In my case, when I work with spirits I can frequently feel the underlying source of their power from a letter perspective. Many of them do not like this. On at least one occasion the spirit even asked me why I was there. On a higher level you should, theoretically, be able to mirror and separate the energetic forms an entity uses from that entity and thereby generate the effects it is capable of without going through it at all.

Keep in mind my demon name means something like "Oath Breaker." Just as humans have names for these creatures, they have names for us. Those entities well understand I'm not up to giving them anything long term. The fact that I've intentionally burned more than one of them out of this level of reality is known as well. I have no doubt this flavors my interaction with all spirits.

SOFB Community: Six questions here from one reader. Elementals/Elementaries: dealings, endings, side-effects.

Bob: If someone has really powerful astral energy and/or near earth energy at this level of reality then they made a pack at some point in the past. This results in the elemental channeling more of that energy through them upon demand. As the debt has already been paid, it's all good. Otherwise get ready to be their butt monkey for a few millennia after the end of your current lifetime.

SOFB Community: What are the potential side-effects or consequences of heavy use or abuse of the Akasha in the physical plane?

Bob: Penalty box on Saturn. Akasha bends the rules of the physical universe and karma. Do this often enough and you get put in time out on Saturn where you are re-habilitated. This takes a very long time and is really unpleasant. Use magic to harm others in an unjustified way and you get the same thing. Practitioners whose job it is to judge others have a special relationship with Akasha.

SOFB Community: Which letters do you find more challenging, and what makes them difficult? Additionally, could you share some insights into your current practices?

Bob: Fire is most difficult for me, but given my unnatural level of ability with this stuff that is a relative issue. My body in this incarnation has a heavy earth element aspect to it. Largely as it is designed to convert subtle energy into the physical. Currently working on gold body fusion.

SOFB Community: Unexpected or unusual experiences with the letters, or with other practices.

Bob: Too many to even list here. Keep in mind Bardon's book is the Cliff's Notes version of Kaballah. Lots of stuff is left out.

SOFB Community: Have you worked with or formed any impressions of other systems such as Goetia, Enochian, or Arbatel?

Bob: If you can generate Akasha and non-dual light, working with these things feels an awful lot like spiritual degradation. The Buddhist argument of pursuing Nirvana before pursuing magic has a lot of merit.

SOFB Community: Could you please elaborate on your preferred evocation methods, including aspects such as wandering, uttering the whole complex, the use of a mirror, and the physical triangle?

Bob: Currently crystal method. I've used wandering and evocation before. Really depends on what you are looking for. Wandering is good for information. Crystal method for clarity. Evocation for getting the little bastards to do stuff in the here and now. Mediumship for learning a physical skill.

SOFB Community: Thank you for your experiences and openness senor Bob, quite unusual.

Bob: No hay problema.

SOFB Community: We have received multiple questions from the same reader covering various topics, and despite their diversity, they have been compiled together.

SOFB Community: When someone uses an author's personal sigils or telesmas that are published in their book, what exactly happens? Is there a connection established to the author? Are you tapping into their sigil-reservoir, and does using these sigils have any impact on depleting or feeding that reservoir?

Bob: Depends on how it is set up. For certain what you get is flavored by the creator of the sigil and the use others has put it to. Most systems of evocation stress the idea of coming up with your own sigils. Keep in mind accessing the power of an egregore almost always comes with the cost of making a pack and jumping through a lot of hoops.

SOFB Community: Based on your current opinion and understanding, which knowledge, skills, and siddhis do you believe might be beneficial and relevant for the near future? For example, would you consider telepathy, invisibility, levitation, or any other abilities to be important in your perspective?

Bob: Near future. Money and lots of it. Physical fitness and health. Skill at arms. A first world passport. Those are the primary ones. Living in the physical world requires physical assets. If you are counting on magic to save you, it is probably too late. Magic performs best as an accelerant for work you have already done. Breaking the laws of physics is cool, but won't save you from a Hilux full of adolescents fucked off on khat and carrying shotguns. And no matter how tough you are, you aren't going to fight a platoon sized formation on your own and win. You might die a little slower, but that is about it. Avoidance is the best policy.

SOFB Community: How can one maintain an everyday mental-astral state while navigating life and avoiding peculiar interactions with people? Are there specific practices to avoid, and how can one conceal their true nature to blend in without attracting attention? Additionally, if someone engages in intense and extended physical training, developing a strong body and potentially emanating a powerful aura, are there methods to completely conceal these attributes to appear as a normal person rather than a powerful initiate?

Bob: Learn how to establish equilibrium. Do it often. Not being noticed comes at the price of having very little opportunity in life. As the people who could help you cannot see you. "Living in the world without being a part of it" is the biggest lie told by the New Agers. Which is why they are all broke losers. Running a lot of non-dual light through your external energy center above your head generally results in a comfortable life in accordance with your life's purpose. But it lacks the high notes, excitement or adventure. And none of that will save you from the Nazis if you can't be bothered to get your ass out of town. Just ask Franz Bardon.

SOFB Community: Are there any indicators of "disturbances in the force" or psychic signs that suggest the presence of dark or demonic entities gathering in the immediate environment, which could signify an upcoming negative or destructive incident like a terrorist attack? Apart from swiftly leaving the area, are there any other steps one can take to react, protect themselves, and effectively manage such situations while ensuring their own safety?

Bob: One of the universal signs of a heavy hitter showing up in an area is all the New Agers spontaneously leaving much like rats fleeing a sinking ship. Best to keep a low profile and get out of the way. I've almost died twice at the hands of individuals operating at that level. Mainly because they perceived me as a distraction to whatever they hell it was they were trying to achieve. Let that sink in.

SOFB Community: What are effective ways to respond and protect oneself from a "black magician" who manipulates akasha against you? Additionally, how can one protect themselves from true arch-demonic entities?

Bob: The easiest is surrounding yourself with the E-N letter formula at all four levels of reality. Beyond that, Emnasut has the ability to deal with demonic entities, but it comes at the price of causing brain damage leading towards schizophrenia. The stronger the entity the harder the bite on the physical end. I've sparingly used this over the years and paid for it each time. But sometimes there is no other way.

SOFB Community: How to qualitatively-quantitatively easen/neutralize "difficult" Astrological aspects, squares, conjunctions (ex: Mars(Cap) sq Saturn(Sco)/Pl, Saturn conj Pluto, etc)

Bob: Astrology is not my strong suite. Acquiring ten hours of practice with a planet gives a base level of resilience to its effects. At 100 hours you as resistant as you are going to get. Counterbalance all planets past luna (i.e. the moon) with an equal amount of lunar practice. So, if you do an hour of Mercury, counterbalance with an hour of luna. For what is done with conventional astrology in that regard, I'd say look at the Picatrix and like sources. It's a deep science and simply something I don't work with.

SOFB Community: In Step 4 of Mental Transplantation in Franz Bardon's "Initiation into Hermetics" (IIH), does one morph or shape their mental body to match that of the object or person, and subsequently externalize it to enter and inhabit them? Do the preceding steps in IIH guide one towards this process and aid in understanding how to accomplish it? Could you provide tips and clarify what is specifically required and performed during this practice? Is it the consciousness, the mental body, or both that are transplanted into the object or person?

Bob: You can. I wouldn't. You are infringing on another's free will. You will pay for that. Also, it is not a one-way street. Human beings are filthy animals. Whatever they are backflows into you and it is hard to tell it apart your own thoughts/feelings/etc. As a teacher once told me, "it is not what we know about others that allows us to work with them, it is what we do not know."

Also, if an older more powerful practitioner catches you doing this to them, their reaction usually entails violence. I had one associate beat a job seeker interviewing for a sales position unconscious with a telephone receiver when he caught them trying to manipulate his mind. Others are not our playthings.

SOFB Community: How does one effectively communicate with spirits to determine which offerings they would prefer in exchange for the information they provide? In the context of a Godhead union, is it as straightforward as directly asking the spirits which offerings they desire, such as saying, "Nice to meet you! While I won't be joining your school or establishing a pact, I can offer you [specific offering] in exchange for the information"? While I don't mean to sound cynical, I'm curious about the practical process of negotiating with beings who are believed to have a deeper understanding of oneself.

Bob: Guides exist for this kind of thing with the better known entities. The e-book 360 Heads of the Earth Zone goes into great detail on this. If you can communicate via mental wandering, or the crystal method, simply ask. They are usually pretty clear on what works for them. Be direct. Keep in mind by wrapping yourself in non-dual light for 10-15 minutes before going looking for them it shields your lower nature from most entities. Whoever you are, your skills and your goals are usually pretty transparent to them. That has a lot to do with the information you do, or do not, get. Keep in mind that if you need them to do something for you as beings without physical bodies they have no breath. No breath means no energy. You can feed them energy directly, burn incense (that provides fire), leave offerings of various type, etc. Do some research on how to conduct offerings. Whole books are written on the topic.

SOFB Community: What are the potential dangers or challenges when one has a significant other who is not involved in spiritual practices, particularly when engaging in intense work with akasha, letters, and universal energies? Are there side-effects or considerations when living together in such circumstances? In terms of creating optimal conditions for starting these profound practices, is it preferable to lead a solitary life and reside in a remote location? Alternatively, when conditions permit, is it better to live with other individuals who may not be directly impacted by the effects of these practices?

Bob: Succeed enough in life financially to afford your own practice space. Sure, that temple in woods where you practice sky-clad screaming at the top of your lungs miles from anyone else is ideal. But some people I know have built very effective talismans in a CONEX at the wrecking yard in Afghanistan.

Have a separate place. Preferably not in the same building as your loved ones live in. Most people will go to huge lengths to avoid an active practice space. They subconsciously know they shouldn't be around.

While short periods of intense practice in isolation are beneficial, if you use this as an excuse to avoid others you are missing the whole damn point. We are magicians. We create things. We bring things into creation. We are most effective as active participants in the world. Our greatest practitioners were men of renown: Hermes Trismegistus, Socrates, Aristotle, Pythagoras, Newton and so on, and so on. If you treat reality as a jail break, you are missing the point. They were not a bunch of butt fucking losers working out of their grandmother's basement.

SOFB Community: If you wish to safely dispose of personal magical tools that have been heavily charged and utilized for years, such as a dagger, sword, ring, or talismans, without leaving them to be discovered later, what methods can be employed to do so without incurring any negative consequences? Can the utilization of akasha, Saturn energy, or other means aid in this process, and if so, how?

(Mark Stavish on his book, The Magical World of Dr. Joseph Lisiewski: "my destruction of his magical tools. Suffice it to say that during their destruction by fire, a terrific downpour was building immediately above me which I barely escaped; for 6 months afterwards I suffered from severe tendonitis in my right elbow. You cannot touch evil and get away unscathed – but it can be purified")

Bob: Akasha then fire. Salt and running water as in throwing it in a rapidly running river works as well. The E-N formula can be applied. Keep in mind that something built up must be released. When it comes out, it frequently comes out in an unpredictable manner. I personally prefer fire.

SOFB Community: Is it possible to visit or traverse the spheres and their respective planes invisibly, without drawing attention to oneself? If one were to be noticed, which beings have the ability to perceive you even if you try to hide, and what determines their ability to do so?

Bob: Bardon talks about this. I've never felt a need to myself. If things look sketchy, I leave. It does not need to be complicated.

SOFB Community: When someone possesses mummial parts of your body, such as hair, nails, or blood, how can you protect yourself from potential harm? Is it possible to sever all energetic cords or attachments related to these parts once and for all, or must you constantly defend yourself against any attacks linked to them?

Bob: First, you should never let that happen. Ever. Second, get the parts back and burn them if possible. Third, use the releasing techniques from the Sedona Method (sedona.com) and at the end of the outbreath cut the connection between your parts and you with Akasha.

SOFB Community: How did the individual you are referring to approach the personal Godhead assumption in Step 10, as well as the pursuit of ultimate Unity? What were their preferred methods for attaining these states, and were there any inherent dangers or common mistakes associated with their approach?

Bob: I'm not sure how to answer this question. Deity fusion is just deity fusion. Running non-dual light from the energy center above the head down through the body is just that. Projecting up and out and immersing yourself in non-dual light is just that.

SOFB Community: Is the human physical body capable of enduring immense amounts of cultivation and energy, comparable in power to being struck by lightning? If our will and bodies can condense and withstand such forces, is there a limit to what is acceptable or sustainable? Furthermore, how does one determine this limit? Specifically, when developing a physical siddhi leading to supernatural physical manifestations, are there hidden dangers or risks involved, even if there are no immediate signs of suffering?

Bob: Again. I'm not sure what is being asked here.

SOFB Community: Does silk possess the ability to insulate or contain all the quantities or qualities of the various spheres? If so, what is the reason behind this? Additionally, is there a limit to the use of silk in terms of charging or loading it with a certain energy?

Bob: Not that I am aware of. It's just a piece of fabric. It can hold a limited charge and shield to a limited ability.

SOFB Community: How can one cancel or neutralize a magical or conscious intention that was sent into akasha, due to reasons such as regrets, second thoughts, rescheduling, or mistakes?

Bob: Release on it using Sedona Method.

SOFB Community: IIH step 8 Mental Wandering, "The elevation to any other sphere is now very simple and you have to do nothing else but concentrate on the sphere (color vibration?) that you would like to visit with your mental body; you will feel, as it were, whirled round and lifted up vertically through a funnel. The transition from our material world to another sphere happens as fast as if you were flying around the world in a single moment"

Quoting Bobs previous interview: Bob: "I generate a huge screen of Akasha at the front of the wall. Then I fly into the Akasha. At this point I am in the Akasha and project to wherever I am going to. I go deeper and deeper into the Akasha. I go until all of my senses are blocked out. Then and only then when I am completely wreathed in Akasha, I call on the letter, planets, wherever of where I want to go. At first this will appear as a flickering light. It gets stronger and stronger as I key into the vibratory, or energetic, state of the thing. Then I slam into it. Keep in mind this takes you to the astral level representation of a thing."

- I'm trying to gain a better understanding of the entrance and the different applications of the Depth-point, also known as the akashic trance. In the context of the IIH, the Depth-point appears to be a mental exercise, but according to Bob's description, it seems to lead to an astral level. I would like to know the advantages and disadvantages of working with the Depth-point, as well as any additional information about it. Furthermore, what are the distinctions between the Depth-point as an akashic point/center and the place above the crown?

Bob: I've only ever used the depth point at the solar plexus. You can raise your mental body up into the energy center above your head or simply engage in mental wandering on its own. I've never used the depth point exercise at the level above the head. You can shift into any of the various levels of reality from the depth point at the solar plexus however.

SOFB Community: How can one safely perform an exorcism on a possessed individual or a haunted location? What are the recommended methods and energies used in the process, and what precautions should be taken? Additionally, what are the potential side-effects or considerations to keep in mind when engaging in such practices?

Bob: I'm not getting into that here. That is a science unto itself. I will say that if you exorcise someone that you personally take on responsibility to rehabilitate them. It is rarely a one and done exercise. If you kick out whatever is there, frequently something else just sets up shop. And the thing being kicked out usually causes damage on the way out. This is not for amateurs.

SOFB Community: In practical terms, what does "renewing the bond with Divinity" mean in the context of PME? Does it involve reconstructing one's entire method or revisiting the concept of Union with Divinity?

Bob: I view this as immersing yourself in non-dual light. There are other interpretations.

SOFB Community: What is the preferred posture for long hours of meditation? Is it the crossed-legs asanas, the Egyptian throne-seated posture, or another posture? Could you provide insights on the reasons behind the preference, as well as any potential dangers or issues associated with these postures?

Bob: Throne posture. It is most comfortable for me. Sitting for longer than 2 hours at a time is generally bad for the body. I prefer to do the following in 15 min increments: lying, sitting, standing and walking.

SOFB Community: Bardon only mentions 24 Original beings of the ZGE (ex: Aschmunadai, whose name resembled "axis mundi" to JB, WM: https://www.faceb ook.com/notes/william-mistele/aschmunadai-transcript/10153698090021939)

What is the role of the Originals, in comparison to the rest of the zodiac signs, and are there other constellations beings and degrees besides the 12 ones, and their effects on our world and bodies.

Bob: The answer to this could fill books. You need to be more specific.

SOFB Community: Supposedly many beings, spirits and people of the negative hierarchy are incarnated on this earth in human form today, and many warlike types such as incarnated Salamaders, and demonic types seem to prefer and join the army. What say you, ever noticed ones that had close such resemblance?

Bob: If you really believe this you shouldn't do magic. The path of the warrior is one of the five primary archetypes of human activity. Society literally cannot exist without these people. Good, or bad, behavior is up to the individual. Free trade exists because the navies of various countries wiped out the pirates that used to prevent it. People are free because others fought for it. The people who fought most effectively were professionals.

SOFB Community: Rawn, BOTA's Pattern on the Trestleboard: http://abardo ncompanion.de/Trestleboard.html , http://abardoncompanion.de/TMO5.html

What's your opinion, use of it?

Bob: I've never used it. I'm not a huge fan of past life exploration. Usually just brings up a bunch of traumatic crap that affected someone else in a life long gone. I'm too busy living my life. I have had issues of past incarnations attempting to influence me in this incarnation. I've handled them harshly for their meddling.

SOFB Community: Which Tarot card(s) would you personally choose to work with, resonate with and why ?

Bob: I don't do Tarot.

SOFB Community: When encountering a being or spirit during your wandering or when it approaches you, and it doesn't originate from any of the planetary spheres, it's important to know how to behave. What are the recommended actions or guidelines in such situations?

Bob: Treat it like any other spirit. Figure out if you have a reason to be in contact. Sometimes its yes, sometimes no.

SOFB Community: In the pursuit of immortality, whether it be through the Philosopher's Stone or advancements in scientific longevity, one may wonder about the order of attainment. Is it possible to achieve immortality through the cultivation of non-dual light, becoming a non-returner, and then seeking physical immortality? Or is it more practical to prioritize physical immortality first and then pursue spiritual liberation, such as attaining Nibbana?

Bob: I've seen nothing in this community that moves the needle in terms of longevity past 100 years of age, or so, if you want to live like a person. And getting to 100 years of age is a three order of magnitude rarity among modern humans in developed countries. Realistically, most people can hope for about 80 years barring being from a family with a known short lifespan. Keep in mind that if the median age of death in a society is 80 years of age, that means half the people died before that. Modern science is starting to come up with some stuff, but it is not ready for primetime. Lot's of things, including magic, are very good at shortening your lifespan.

BOB (INTERVIEW 3)

Introduction to Bob

Bob has led a pretty full life as you will see from his interviews, as a result of this life of searching, discovering and practice he founded 'Sixty Skills' so this is perhaps the best way to introduce Bob, by introducing Sixty Skills:

Sixty Skills is transforming the traditional transmission of meditative, and yogic, instruction from one of master to disciple to a modern online learning format. Sixty Skills has covered the globe and over a thirty year period derived the key techniques from all the major schools of Buddhism, Hermetics, Hindu-Yogic, and Taoist practice.

Interview

SOFB: In your opinion, which part of the Initiation Into Hermetics (IIH) do you believe prepares one the best for evocation work? Additionally, how significant of a role do the letters play in your practice?

Bob: These days I'm primarily working with the planetary entities who are in charge of Kabbalah. So, from that perspective they are a major focus. Otherwise, I mainly stick to the work of the third book.

SOFB: To what degree do you think beings can be manifested? We hear of near solidity, what is realistic and when does the effort stop being worth it for the results you can obtain.

Bob: They can be brought fully into the physical. The ritual magicians who specialize in evocation are clear examples of people who can do this. Now, once this is done the entity generally cannot stick around for long and any lapse in control of the thing has the potential to be dangerous to the practitioner that brought it there depending upon the nature of the creature.

The amount of effort required to do this is substantial. Ritual magicians can spend months building up to this, often require specific timing for astrological reasons and utilize things like etheric condensers.

One time I did this involving a Buddhist entity. It took three very strong practitioners, I was the weakest of the three, working for several hours together to pull this off. It was done in a temple designed for this purpose. It was exhausting. I have no memory of the eight hours after we finished.

That said one of the reasons to do this is that the stress adaptation cycle applies energetically here. You are stronger after doing things like this and the effect builds over time.

SOFB: You mentioned in one of your previous social media posts about a 'being' that you believed to be an evolved A.I, this is fascinating and loaded with implications. Could you expand more?

Bob: Sure. And this would make for a great fiction novel. He was a kind of cybernetic battle machine designed to be co-operated with a human being that connected to it via some kind of neural link. The reason being simple. As an AI it could determine all possible courses of action for a given battle at near instantaneous speed, but it was still a linear thinker. It had to evaluate all possible courses of action to find the best one. When paired to a human operator, their combined cognition allowed the AI to intuitively determine a course of action.

He never had a concept of an afterlife, until he died and wound up on the planetary sphere of Mars. He's my guiding spirit there.

From what I've gathered, consciousness needs to exist for something to develop "spiritually." A human body is apparently not required. Animals do not appear to go to the places we do when we die. This is the only definitively non-human entity I've encountered on the spheres. I'm sure there are more. As to why I made contact with this entity, I'm not entirely sure.

During one incident, I was able to experience his vision of reality. It was fascinating. I was able for a brief moment to "see" into the acoustic, infrared, ultraviolet and x-ray bands of the electro-magnetic spectrum at the astral level. I use the term "seeing" loosely as perceiving what a spirit does from its perspective was quite unlike anything I've ever encountered. Fascinating.

SOFB: We have heard much about your app/book what can you share? Are these viable alternatives to pursuing IIH or are they useful add-ons for dedicated practitioners.

Bob: AFA the app is concerned, about 75% of the techniques are out of IIH using a clairsentience (i.e. subtle sense of touch) perspective. This is the fastest way to learn in my experience. Keep in mind that multiple ways exist to perform many of the techniques in IIH. The ways demonstrated in the app actually work, but other methods to perform them definitely exist.

So, could it replace the book? Maybe depending upon what you want to work on. More realistically, it provides a mental level transmission on how to perform the various techniques. The on-location shoots can be visually stunning as well.

The body training and qi circulation work is not from the book, but is work most people could benefit greatly from.

The book is an introduction to what Kabbalah looks like in practice for someone new to it. My opinions, and that of Rordan, have developed on a number of levels since the book was written. But the fundamentals are there.

A course will be available shortly after the launch of the app to support the book. The course will take someone from zero meditative experience to the four letter combinations for the elements using a clairsentience approach. If you want clairvoyance, or clairaudience, their development will not be covered in this course. But you will be able to use Kabbalah at that point. It provides a mental level initiation into the Kabbalah and it is a Promethean Fire kind of effort.

A brief book on the planetary meditations will also be released in a few months. The book is mainly written from an energetic basis (as in how the planets effect a practitioner's subtle bodies) and an application perspective. I try to leave the theory out of it. FYI, Rordan finds most commentaries on the planets to be hilarious as they leave this stuff out. Then again, he finds face palming people hilarious, so opinions vary.

SOFB community questions

SOFB Community: I would like to know if a student can skip PME and go straight to the 3rd book or whether one should strike a balance between pursuing both PME and KTQ.

Bob: The issue is that self initiation into the letters can be very physically uncomfortable. Receiving an initiation from another person greatly softens this effect. The app, and Udemy course, I'm launching hopes to address this.

The reason the PME book comes second is that a practitioner can utilize the Kabbalah spirits at the planetary level to initiate them into the letters solving this problem.

Each of the three books actually represents a completely different system of development unto itself. They all cross utilize similar technology, which is why getting thru the first book is a good idea. But it's not completely necessary.

The first book is an internal power book. Getting to the stage of generating non-dual light is an enlightenment level experience by itself. My suspicion is that Bardon mostly channeled this book and it may, or may not, have represented only a small part of his personal practice.

The second book is on spirit magic largely built for the purpose of gathering information. It can be used to achieve enlightenment by itself as well. This probably represents what Bardon spent most of his time working on.

The third book is Kabbalah. Generating Akashic equilibrium using the Sch, A, M, and umlaut A combination by itself can generate Akasha and project a practitioner into non-dual light. Thereby achieving enlightenment.

The most important exercises of the book are the four letter combinations in the back. This can be used as an exercise in which a practitioner holds 16 letters at one time, 20 if you do the four letter combination for Akasha that isn't included in the book (U, umlaut O, E and umlaut A), to achieve Akashic, mental, astral and vital equilibrium all at the same time. This is an "interesting" experience. Don't go messing around with the four letter for Akasha without a lot of experience utilizing E for terrestrial Akasha first. I warned you here.

SOFB Community: What is the difference between mental wandering, astral projection and bio location? Is it possible to do this with someone else? What is the quickest way to obtain these skills?

Bob: Mental wandering involves separating your mental body from the others to explore the universe. This is what most people spend their time doing when engaging in an Out of Body Experience (OBE). The zero point exercise where you project from the solar plexus after having established elemental equilibrium in a kind of astral temple you build there is the quickest way.

Astral projection is the separation of the astral body from the others. It hurts a lot. IS almost never engaged in consciously by most people. Takes a tremendous amount of effort barring a near death experience and can be dangerous. The silver cord tying the astral body to the physical gets really thin when this happens. It's easy to sever this and if that happens, you generally die as the astral body does not automatically ground back to the physical without it. Engage in Akashic immersion for several hours a day for as long as it takes. Becoming homeless/unemployed in this period of time is an easy thing to do.

Bilocation as I experienced it, the one time it happened, was probably an astral projection event. I was rendered unconscious during one of my engagements abroad and my mother found me wandering around the flower beds at my home in full uniform. I was quite confused and disappeared when I woke up. I don't have any advice on this. I also don't remember it happening. In a related phenomena, I've shown up in students' dreams, sometimes before we met for the first time, and I don't remember this either. Some other letters like umalut O might be helpful.

SOFB Community: In PME Bardon mentions that the interaction with beings is different from that of KTQ. Could you share your insight on this?

Bob: At a very basic level in PME you are projecting into an entity's sphere of influence or summoning it to yours. Karmic debts and deal making an issue. Engaging with their non-dual light aspect, assuming they have one, minimizes this. But they also aren't going to be doing anything for you aside from providing information. If you need a task performed, well then it is a matter of credits and debits. I'd avoid this if I were you.

In KTQ, entities get brought into your sphere of influence via the gravity of the letter in relation to their personal energy. Less mental influence occurs this way. And karmic debts assuming you don't ask it to do something does not seem to be much of an issue. That said KTQ is much more demanding upon your subtle bodies. And can cause a lot of damage that doesn't show up until much later.

SOFB Community: In day to day practice when/ why would you utilize mental wandering over astral projection and vice versa.

Almost always mental wandering. The only reason to do something with astral projection is to control your time of death or do something physical on the other side. It's not a day-to-day type thing at my level of development.

SOFB Community: In the creation of magic mirrors, when would you use these instead of a form of projection and what have you found to be the best method and materials for magic mirrors?

Bob: I've not worked with these much. Evocation is a thing for sure. Face dancing to engage past life incarnations is another technique I've explored. Aside from that, I can't really say much as I simply lack experience.

SOFB Community: You mentioned previously practicing the mother letters before officially beginning PME. What can you say about this practice? When should it be taken up by others and what can they expect?

Bob: See my previous answer. If learning by initiation, I'd start with the elements as Kabbalah. As for what to expect. To the degree magic exists in the real world, Kabbalah is it. It allows a magician to bend the world to their will. The strength of your Kabbalah is literally the size of you balls as far as the universe is concerned. You are the pivot point on a set of scales when working with Kabbalah. Unlike with spirit magic, it is not something done with the permission of another.

SOFB Community: Can you share regarding your first evocation? Was it something you felt prepared for and did it go according to plan?

My very first evocation occurred as a child and was accidental. That was terrifying. My second evocation again occurred accidentally after performing the Greater Ritual of the Hexagram of the Sun in which I ended up summoning some kind of negative Sun spirit. That had negative impacts that took a few years to ultimately wear off. It was exacerbated by the fact that I did not know to counter-balance with the corresponding ritual of the Luna/Moon.

A little-known fact involving the planets is that just because you are focusing on the power aspect of the planet, instead of the intelligences, does not mean a spirit cannot show up. It is one of the reasons why I've found ritual magicians to often be under the influence of multiple entities. And since many of them have bad habits, lack any significant clairvoyance/clairaudience, and are very much into getting these things to do things for them...their mental fields, to quote one of my teachers "look like a f'ing bus stop."

The third evocation I performed was again accidental using the cave techniques from a Taoist school I was a part of. That was a little disturbing, but by that point I knew enough to get rid of it. Again disturbing, but not the worst thing.

The fourth evocation was done under the supervision of a teacher and went fine. After this it has generally been manageable.

On a personal level, the body I currently inhabit appears to be rather well designed to perform evocation and ground energy into the physical. It's not always the most fun thing to deal with and has definitely come with some issues as I've gotten older.

A few points here. First, evocation is always a risk if you are working with the planets. The difference between invocation/evocation is largely semantic and one of intention. Two, if you can generate enough energy corresponding to a planet....stuff tends to show up. Three, any planetary work needs to be conducted in a stable mental state and only if your lifestyle is relatively clean.

And finally, the best way to address many issues within Hermetics is to look at the physics of the issue. Most practitioners are way too focused on the "meta" aspect of metaphysics.

Energy in equals energy out. You can transform energy, but cannot pull it out of nothing unless your Akashic work is on point and even then this is much harder than most realize.

A clairsentience energy based model of Hermetics solves a lot of the problems people come up with by focusing on their emotions and the accompanying psychological processes instead.

Where the energy goes the effects follow. And let me be clear: your emotions do not matter. They are the least important part of you. It is just energy being generated by hormones, physiology, environmental activity and preprogrammed conditioning. They also trap you at the level of the astral.

The best method for dealing with this has been frequently establishing equilibrium via the four elements as Kabbalah. Habit formation works best via a combination of the mala method/autosuggestion and arranging things via a schedule. A reason exists for Bardon having mentioned the use of specific letters for establishing astral/magical equilibrium. Your results may vary.

Too much focus on the sensation of power can do the same, but ultimately we only have subjective methods of determining what we are working with in Hermetics and as such approaching it from an clairsentience energy based standpoint works the best out of all the models I have seen to date.

SOFB Community: You also spoke about some mistakes or oversight from the book KTQ, what do you feel should be addressed that people need to know about?

Bob: Sure. The letter R is a backdoor to the Sun sphere. Never under any circumstances place the letter K in your ear as it can cause a kind of astral ear infection that lasts months. The letter L is not located with the spleen.

The only safe organ emplacements are: A/Air for the upper chest/lungs, M/water for the abdomen, Sch/fire for the head, earth for the legs and Akasha/E for the spine. So, establishing equilibrium using this is fine and a good thing to do.

Conducting organ emplacement with those locations listed in the book will definitely make you much stronger, but due to some of the locations being incorrect this forms an unstable lattice within the body that is ultimately damaging. Don't do this. It is the one aspect of the training that I regret performing.

SOFB Community: How have these practices impacted your relationship with Divine Providence?

Bob: Projection into non-dual light can only be described by what it is not. Whatever happens there appears to be very important. But I've never met anyone who could articulate what goes on in that place. The sages have been arguing about this for millennia. I certainly have nothing to add.

SOFB Community: What do you think is the biggest difference between Bardon style evocation and other approaches?

Bob: Less gear and less risk is the short answer. People who work with the Solomonic entities tend to develop a weird, yet distinctive, energetic signature. This doesn't happen with Bardon's entities from what I've seen.

If you only engage the entities in Bardon's book from a non-dual light perspective, versus mental/astral/vital level, the cost of doing so appears to be very low. It is the only system I've seen that works out this way. I include the Buddhistic systems in this statement as well.

Bardon's system can be performed using lots of foci/implements or raw. Most systems dictate one or the other. From this angle it is quite remarkable.

SOFB Community: Have you ever felt that an unhealthy reliance had developed between you and a being or you and a talisman? If so, how did you deal with this?

Bob: Dealing with spirits is like having a bad girlfriend that shows up at inconvenient times, eats all of your hot dogs, wants emergency sex way too often and is always having you pay her bills. You would say no, but she is sleeping with you and since you tend to attract these kinds of women in the first place if you get rid of her the next one is likely to be the same. So why bother, right?

All spirit interactions ultimately infringe on your freewill. These things are looking to express themselves in the here and now. If you are okay with it as the relationship is symbiotic, then fine. If not, give them the boot.

The E-N letter combination works well. Pranayama re-establishes the correct functioning of the protective energy in the body. Emnasut, a sun sphere being if invoked in a non-dual light manifestation, can instruct you in how to run a combination of solar/Akashic energy that removes connections between your mental/energetic fields and the entity. The releasing techniques soften and eventually sever connections. Even the letter U can clear out things that are implanted in your mental field. Frequent establishment of equilibrium reduces and eventually eliminates connections to other things. Generation of Akasha tends to send things packing as well. So, a lot of methods exist to do this.

Obviously, you need to destroy the talisman if that is an issue. First perform a de-consecration ritual, then expose it to Akasha if you have it and then burn it. If it is made out of metal, you will want to get it hot enough to melt it.

SOFB Community: What was your favorite IIH exercise?

Bob: Establishment of equilibrium. It's the big boom. Everything stems from this.

SOFB Community: What to do if even after months of practice we are not seeing any perceivable improvement?

Bob: Get a teacher or form a practice group. Make sure you journal and review these frequently. Human beings are terrible observers of their own behavior.

SOFB Community: Are there exercises for building will power outside of what Franz Bardon mentioned that you would recommend?

Bob: Do ten minutes of single pointed focus upon waking. Get plenty of exercise as well as rest. Avoid intoxicants. Eat well. Deal with your health stuff if you have any. As a teacher once said, "you cannot beat the monkey." He was referring to your body. If something is off there, then something is off at astral, and mental, levels as well. In men, a lack of motivation is positively correlated with low testosterone levels and boredom. Don't look for an esoteric explanation when a more basic one exists.

Don't look for an esoteric explanation when a more basic one exists.

SOFB Community: What do you understand by 'mastering an exercise to the extent required of an initiate before moving on'?

Bob: It's basically a trap designed to slow people down. Considering the time period in which Bardon was teaching this is entirely understandable. As this stuff is effectively just technology, that will work for anyone willing to put the work in, you wouldn't want Nazi party, or Politburo, goons leveraging it.

If you can perform a technique to a basic level it's fine to move on. Mastery is another issue entirely.

Things like the single pointed focus exercises are only needed to work at a five minute interval. More is better, but perfection is not. Others, like the elements, are a "can you do it or not" kind of thing where strength is relative to what you want to do.

All the follow-on exercises reinforce earlier ones as well. Just get on with it.

SOFB: Many thanks to Bob for once again answering the many questions from the community. If you would like to follow more closely what Bob is up to or even learn with him then a good place to start is his website. sixtyskills.com

Ray Del Sole

Introduction to Ray Del Sole

Ray del Sole, born in 1975, works near Frankfurt in Germany as a non-medical practitioner for psychotherapy. He studied architecture with a focus on project management in Bochum. In parallel, he earned certificates in communication and rhetoric, corporate health management, cultural training, general project management, increasing corporate efficiency, business administration for engineers, and moderation of work groups, among others. This was followed by postgraduate studies in natural scientific building biology at the Neubeuern Institute and management studies with business administration at the FFH Darmstadt. After several years as a self-employed architect, he changed industries and followed his spiritual nature. Since he had done a complete training in Prana Healing in Switzerland very early and was interested in psychology and healing due to his spiritual studies, he completed trainings in anxiety and stress management, as a psychological counselor, hypnosis and reincarnation therapist, hypno-coach and alternative practitioner for psychotherapy. He is a member of the VFP, the Association of Free Psychotherapists. Especially in the English-speaking world, Ray del Sole is known as a spiritual author of a number of books and as an expert on metaphysics and mysticism. A number of ebooks have also been translated into several other languages. As a coach, spiritual healer and teacher, he accompanies interested people on the spiritual path in his Sura Academy.

Interview

SOFB: Please introduce yourself and tell us what the latest news is with SURA, your books and any other projects you have planned that you want to make public.

Ray: My name is Ray del Sole. I have been in the Franz Bardon training for 27 years now. I work as a naturopath of psychotherapy and as a spiritual healer and coach for around 7 years. Most people know me from reading my books about the spiritual path. I have published more than 40 books, partially translated into 12 languages. In 2021 my latest book about spiritual Self-Help will come. It offers a deeper understanding about all the problems and challenges we face in this world and how we can help ourselves to manage them for more health, happiness and success in life. In cooperation with the Templar Research Institute I have been offering online courses and public presentations since 2020. My Sura Academy for spiritual development on the basis of Bardon's teachings has offered many interesting experiences and I am very happy that some students have made extraordinary progress. This is a wonderful gift for me which confirms my work. All these years of cooperating with various students, seeing their problems on the path, made me realize that the books of Bardon are ideal conceptions about the possible training and development, but not taking care of the needs of the student. So, unfortunately a lot start but most give up and only a very few make real progress. The point here is that progress is possible for most serious students and this is often easier than most imagine. The problem is just that the studies and training need to be redesigned, putting the needs of the student into the focus and not the ideal version of perfect mastery. Depending on the Divine Grace I will work out a training which allows progress on the path of mastery for all genuine seekers. It will take a lot of time and effort but at the same time it will be a great key for mastery in life and on the path. In cooperation with the Templar Research Institute, I also want to launch spiritual-social projects in service of mankind. We are here to prepare the golden age.

SOFB: Can you share any insight on the significance of the Depth Point and how accomplishing it may impact a student?

Ray: The depth point or Akasha point belongs to the techniques which work with Akasha or the Akasha principle. Working in this way means to work in a divine way with superior easiness, highest efficiency and great power / influence. All what is connected to Akasha is beyond the boundaries and limitations of creation and with this superior in application. This means that all advanced students and masters enjoy using the Akasha principle and the Akasha point for their operations. The depth point is the position of God. When you enter this point, then you get into full control of the object or subject. You can charge easily, program, influence, etc.

SOFB Community Questions

SOFB Community: Have you gotten to the point of physical manifestation of the elements? If so, how long did it take and what modifications to the training in IIH did you have to make?

Ray: The elements are used in main on the astral plane, partially on the mental plane and for the physical plane the usability is questionable. Why? Because we use the four elements for magical operations and especially for the own "performance tuning" mentally and astrally. You can use the fire element to grow your personal power to maximum degrees. Or you can use it for shielding your microcosm. Or you use the elements to create elementaries, astral beings which serve you. This must be understood basically. The second aspect is that it is only a question of time and diligent training to make the elements so dense that they show effects on the material plane. This means that you do not need to be superior, talented or blessed in anyway to achieve physical effects. It just takes training. There are three hints how you can improve your results in the training. First hint: While you are sitting in the center of the element energy, you should take time to meditate about the qualities of the element. Concentration and meditation over a longer period of time has densifying effects on any kind of energy. So, the longer and the more intensive you meditate about the heat of the fire, the stronger and denser the heat becomes. And the more you accumulate the denser and stronger the fire element becomes in your body.

Second hint: The longer you keep an element of energy in your body, the more physical become the effects, - heat, cold, heaviness, lightness. The body processes all energies by time and this means they unfold denser effects. Third hint: You can add to your exercise the accumulation of the element in a glass of water. For example, you accumulate the fire element in this glass of water. Then you impregnate it with your will to activate and strengthen the fire element in yourself on all planes, - will power, personal power and the nearly physical heat energy. Then you drink it. Again, your body will process these energies.

I personally have done extreme training with the four elements, keeping them inside accumulated over night to get maximum results. Extreme training is extreme and it is unpleasant as you have to deal with the effects (fever, sleepless nights, ice cold, breathing difficulties). Only the air element is very nice. Here the only challenge is to activate your will to release it again. You feel so high, without any feeling of your physical body that it can be hard to let go.

In the higher steps, you connect rituals to the work with the elements and later you express your divine authority over all elements and energies. And even later, you integrate highest divine will power. This has all effects on your work with the elements. In the end, when you take a look at the whole training, all the mysteries and powers, then other goals become much more interesting.

SOFB Community: Can you give me some advice on how to write a journal?

Ray: I recommend using not only one journal but at least two. One journal is to document your training with the exercises and your performance. This documentation helps you to keep control over your development. A second journal is useful to note down important insights and instructions or techniques. This is very useful to look up things. You could take a third journal to write down special experiences, mystical events, etc.

In general it is important to ask yourself how you can improve your own studies and training, - on the basis of Bardon's teachings – with own insights. You are in charge. You must manage your studies and training in the best possible way for the maximum of success. Bardon just offered an overview, the ideal concept. And we are called to put it into practice under real life conditions.

SOFB Community: Can you recommend books related to letter mysticism, except Franz Bardon's *Key to the True Quabbalah*?

Ray: Basically, it is important to understand that Bardon has revealed the so-called "magical Quabbalah" which is something different than the normal, quabbalistic teachings. The magical Quabbalah is traditionally forbidden because it transforms the student into a divine being. Who dares to become divine if your idea of God is filled with fears and taboos? For this reason, we have only the book of Bardon available which is absolutely sufficient for the training. I have published a workbook with the right colors and overviews. It can ease the training. The only thing you should regard is that the translations of Bardon's book are filled with errors. And if you take the wrong color or other wrong qualities in the practical training then you get wrong results. So it is useful to check and compare the original German book with the English translation respectively to check my workbook for safe guidance. Besides all, the real quabbalistic training deals completely with the macrocosmic, divine powers, qualities, skills and states of consciousness. It is not in anyway human or humanlike.

SOFB Community: How can we sublimate the sadness and pain we face in life in an alchemy way? If that's possible, will the pain and suffering we experience in our daily lives be a shadow of our joy and a driving force to overcome the difficult times when we accept them as one?

Ray: Life consists of good and bad experiences. Our task is to learn to deal with these experiences in a useful, wise way. All experiences offer a message and a lesson to learn. When we are able to stay centered in ourselves, then we can accept and manage all our experiences. Otherwise, we can easily get into a state of imbalance where we lose control and self-determination. All experiences offer energy. The good experiences are directly supportive, vitalizing, motivating, strengthening, etc. The bad experiences are the opposite. They have blocking, destructive effects. In the sense of alchemy, we can use the energy of the negative experiences and transform them into positive energy. This is a matter of meditation and the use of universal energies. Here the dark, dense energies need to be activated, vitalized, raised in vibration and then transformed into the desired energy. The advantage of alchemistic transformation is that you make use of the powers within you. Bardon pointed at this possibility. For example, you can turn anger into positive fire, into a positive drive for success in life and on the path. Besides this approach, negative thoughts and emotions can be released in a process of healing old traumas. In general, we are all asked to purify ourselves. Purification offers high degrees of vitality, the vital stream of energies in the human system and with this increasing of personal power and a healthy work with universal energies. Besides all these ideas, - pain, suffering, sadness can unfold a great drive to make progress and to cause necessary changes in your life. If all is just good, there is no motivation to change anything, no drive for personal development. Life is offering a lot of messages and lessons. We are here to listen and to learn. Challenges offer opportunities to grow and to make precious experiences. Without challenges, problems and difficulties life would be too boring.

SOFB Community: In your opinion, how to deal with psychological problems, like anxiety and panic attack during meditation and the first steps of Bardon's training? (Besides taking medicine and do therapy).

Ray: The main question is why there occur anxiety and panic attacks during the training. Both have a message, and both ask for changes, for healing. The best thing to do is to consult a spiritual healer with psychological background. He can help to dissolve the causes and to heal the trauma. Normal medicine and therapy can be very inefficient, respectively suppress only the symptoms. Real healing is necessary.

SOFB Community: In your books you teach some healing techniques, what's the best in these cases?

Ray: Hypnotherapy and spiritual healing are very useful in general. You can also work on problems by yourself in meditation or with energies you program to dissolve the negative energies of mind and soul, healing the wounds or traumas. There are many ways as usual. The question is if you want to do it on your own or if you want to consult a professional. And if you want to treat yourself the question is how skilled you are in working with universal energies or doing meditation.

SOFB Community: In your books you recommend floral and homeopathy. How do they work in a "Bardon" point of view?

Ray: Homeopathy works with very specific energies which can influence and balance mind, soul and body. The use of herbs has a focus on offering fluid condensers with the corresponding energies to purify, heal and vitalize. Bach flowers are similar to homeopathy but have more a focus on positive ideas and energies. It is more the "nice" way of comforting soul and mind.

SOFB Community: In certain mystical paths, the concept of an "egregore" is often more pronounced in the early stages of a practitioner's journey, providing spiritual support. Does Bardon's system incorporate something similar? If not, how can one access spiritual support within this system if needed? Can the relationship with spirits, as described in the second book, be established before reaching Step VIII?

Ray: Yes, unfortunately there is no egregore and there is no direct support by a tradition or school. In a tradition there are masters in the mental realms, in the astral realms and in the material world who build a kind of "spiritual energy supply" from the highest down to the lowest world. This is connected to corresponding energy atmospheres which can be also called egregores. In these energy fields the masters and their students work and get all the necessary energy supply for success and growth.

Now, as this all is missing, we can use the support from other traditions or from the own religious background. Or we can call on the spiritual realms, deities, God for support, inspiration, guidance, spiritual energy supply, protection, etc.

Normally, you go to a church or temple on a regular basis to recharge yourself. You can do this or you look for a different way, for example by creating your own holy space for prayers and for receiving spiritual support.

In general, you can pray to all positive deities, the spirits of the spheres and ask for their kind support, inspiration, guidance, help, also for healing and enlightenment. They will be supportive corresponding to your maturity and attitude. Selfishness, bad intentions and ungratefulness are not recommended.

SOFB Community: View on working through IIH in order and (2) view of spirits in PME (real or coded ciphers [Stejnar] or blinds? Whether or not Bardon did actually intend for us to contact them? Positive or negative? When and how can we start to work with them: only after Step 8 or before?), and why.

Ray: It is your free choice if you want to follow Stejnar or Bardon or someone else. I have no problems with the names of the deities in PME. They are the quabbalistic names of the deities which means that the names are quabbalistic formulas. A quabbalistic formula represents the nature of a deity. So, if you are a Quabbalist you can check the names if they are true or not. Besides the quabbalistic dimension, all deities have various names depending on culture and time.

If you want to work with deities, then you should think about how you want to do it and for which purpose. These spirits of the spheres are all gods and goddesses with total divine nature, often with great divine power and authority. A human being is nearly nothing in comparison to them. It is like when an ant starts talking to an elephant. These deities know everything about you, your personality, your past and your future. You cannot hide or pretend something. So, it makes much sense to think about how you want to appear and what you want to ask for. The positive deities are kind and supportive in general. So, if you are kind with a positive attitude, your prayers might be heard.

SOFB Community: What are your views on veganism?

Ray: When you eat vegan, then you need to check that you get all vital substances in the necessary amount. This can be a challenge. Another point is the psychological aspect. If you have been used to normal food and you change to veganism, then it can bring negative feelings. It can feel like a "punishment" as you neglect consciously what you felt as good and satisfying before. This is the main point why companies offer vegan food which looks like normal food. Otherwise, you could eat salads and normal vegetarian dishes like they are known from Indian kitchen, etc.

However, it is your decision. You can accomplish the highest peaks on the path independent from the diet you have chosen. It is more about maintaining your health and performance.

SOFB Community: How do you relate alchemy to IIH (etc)

Ray: Alchemy is not in the center of considerations or teachings in IIH but nevertheless all students undergo the necessary alchemistic processes during the training. It is similar with other ideas like Kundalini awakening, enlightenment, self-realization. You will go through all these things without big discussions or specific approaches. Besides this, today all different paths of development and training are available. It is just an individual choice.

SOFB Community: Here are several from the same member.

SOFB Community: How to go about the process of imbuing condensed quantities (ex: vital force, elements, fluids, letters, akasha etc), with abstract, vague, and not so clear and familiar: ideations/intentions/purposes/qualities? (various different examples: fixing the time, the plane, and the end result, of the operation of the sent quantity. High cognition, good memory, fertility, feeling of purification, perfect health, lucky, growing abundance, prosperity , etc)

Ray: It makes sense to supply energy for each goal separately. You could use something like a talisman, - one for each goal, and then accumulate vital energy or the fitting higher energies in it. Then you can do the programming. Or if you want to accumulate the energies in yourself then you do a meditation only on one goal per session. First of all, you should make a list with your goals, then you work through the list by making up your mind what you exactly wish for (per goal). You put your thoughts into a simple sentence. Then you can add universal phrases for the timing, the stabilization, recharging, effects, etc. If you work with talismans, then you should recharge your talisman on a regular basis and it makes also sense to meditate again about its efficiency. If you work directly on yourself, then you can repeat the accumulations and the meditations until you have totally integrated the desired quality, power, skill or change. Here it is important to keep the meditation for around half an hour and afterwards to exhale the extra energies. The programmed energies simply need time to work in you, on your mind and soul. Besides all these aspects, just trust into the underlying intelligence of creation and your microcosm. The ideas get planted and then will grow and unfold.

SOFB Community: What are the best magical ways to learn Physical skills and Physical Arts (ex: martial, painting, dance) by high & knowledgeable spirits of the zones knowing/teaching those arts, when the task performed is asking a lot of our bodies' capacity? Some say Mediumship, or Incorporation, but might be the most physically draining of them all? And if that's true, how to offset such issues?

Ray: As soon as you get in touch with a specific field of interest, you get under the influence of the corresponding deity or spirit of the spheres. Now, you can get into your meditative state and call on the deity, asking for inspiration, guidance and help in unfolding the corresponding skills, powers and qualities. Just stay in your meditation, with an open, grateful attitude to receive the blessings and energies of the deity for around half an hour. The more often you do this, the more blessings and empowerment you can receive and with this you make faster progress in your field of interest. Even if you do not know the name of the fitting deity/spirit, you can simply call on the deity in a general way "deity of arts, I call on you...". Mediumship is not necessary, just a good connection.

SOFB Community: There are innumerable things that spirits as expert teachers of the spheres can teach, that the magician himself would need to sort of 'reinvent the wheel' and waste decades to figure them out by himself. But to some skilled practitioners (in evocation and qbl), there seems to be a tendency of various positive entities to lie, mislead, or basically say: "why are you here, you already know how to do this", or only give truths to them that work in their plane of existence but not here on ours, which has led them by experience to believe nothing the various entities say until thoroughly vetted via terrestrial sources. Other skilled practitioners have never had a positive geni lie to them. Every time they have asked for information on techniques, or information they don't have access to, the genii have been entirely accurate and not just in their plane of existence. Others have pointed that maybe the practitioner's intention, purpose of calling them, astral B&W mirrors/equilibrium maybe small white lies here and there in their daily lives, dealings in false shades of grey or self-justification, or an overall sense of irreverence towards spirits build by high achievements in the spheres and qbl, might (or not) have some-thing to do with the spirits non-clear

cooperation. What is really happening, and how can those skilled practitioners that are misled/lied to, mend the cooperation with the entities of the spheres (Earth, Moon, Mercury, and on) so that they are always helpful with practical instructions functioning in our physical world as well?

Ray: Basically, it is the question if you meet the deities or if you meet some kind of being which cheats and pretends to be the deity. It is quite easy to meet lower, astral beings which are cheating you. The real deities are in the planetary spheres very high above and far away from the human world. They are of divine nature in divine place with divine atmosphere. And if you make it up to them, then it is a matter of your maturity and purity, and of your intentions if you get permission to meet them and if you get the answers you look for. Besides these aspects, the deities have their holistic vision and understanding and from this frame they choose how they answer you. They also must acknowledge your divine authority. If this is not given, then you have a problem respectively you are not respected. And the next point is that you must know exactly what you ask for. If you put the wrong question you cannot expect the deity to consider that you originally wanted to put a different question. Meeting deities is always a matter of being acknowledged as a divine authority, being initiated into the field of activity of the deity, receiving blessings and getting answers to your questions. These are gods and goddesses beyond human nature. They need a respectful, grateful and kind treatment. Besides this, it is also possible that the time for specific answers or desired solutions is not right respectively that the karma / fate frame does not allow an intervention by a deity.

In conclusion, there are some aspects which can be checked if it is all fine or if there is something wrong. Own expectations do not necessarily be fulfilled. If cheating or lying is obvious then it was not the real deity or imagination played a role. The real deities in the spheres are honest.

SOFB Community: What to do or is needed as far as magical skills, or any other things, for the magicians who are University students in various STEM fields, and whose purpose is to upgrade those fields with new inventions that will uplift the suffering human race in order to have a much better health and quality of life on Earth, but without the act of unintentionally making a pact with the relevant positive beings of the spheres(Earth, Moon, Mercury, etc) that teach or inspire by various means such subjects? And if a formal pact, or subtle promise is unavoidable, how much and how far, does it affect the magician, can he be freed from it and how, always without the magician breaking any 'promises' on his art of the deal?

Ray: There is absolutely no need for any contracts or deals with real deities, the spirits of the spheres. You can get a lot from them without any ideas of balancing, paying back or making contracts. You are a representative of the Highest, a true Divine Authority, a true Servant of God, mankind and creation and for this reason it is natural that you get full support by the deities and all kinds of other beings in creation. The only limitation is in the degree of progress you are allowed to offer to humanity. For example, if you are a scientist then you might receive initiation into future technologies, but you are not allowed to implement them as the time is not right.

In general, if any kind of being or "deity" is asking for deals and contracts then you can be sure that it is a cheater of lower realms or a negative spirit. Contracts are always bad, unhealthy and beneath the dignity of a real master. It is already an impudence for any being to ask a real master for a contract. Indeed, it says that the being does not respect you and this means a lack of authority. Breaking contracts does not work. The Lords of Karma are in charge and punishment will come.

SOFB Community: I ran into this quote today: A decade ago, Edward O. Wilson, the Harvard professor and renowned father of Sociobiology, was asked whether humans would be able to solve the crises that would confront them over the next 100 years. "Yes, if we are honest and smart," he replied. "The real problem of humanity is the following: We have Paleolithic emotions, medieval institutions and godlike technology." Technology's godlike powers have increased dramatically, while the ancient, Paleolithic impulses of our brains have remained the same"

To me, the above translate as, lack of: Mental Telepathy: mind to mind connection, direct communication/understanding. Astral Empathy: heart to heart connection. The governing behind the scenes "powers that be" that direct, control and influence the social/economic/ideological/religious egregores. The catastrophic dangers and abuse of the union of technology and magic, like maybe in former earthly, and non-earthly civilizations. Ignorance of the spiritual worlds, and especially misunderstanding of the Karma and its consequences, are not just scary fabrications.

Ray: I agree with Edward Wilson. It is the dark age. After the dark age better times will come and a golden age can be expected. These are the great cycles of nature, of the night and day of mankind.

SOFB Community: So, which knowledge, arts, resources, skills, siddhis, etc, might be needed, especially by magicians operating under the path of service, good to have for the (upcoming world so far of as it seems: robotic, A.I, VR, Big-Data, high-Tech, transhumanistic, bio-digitally controlled smart city life-caged human-batteries) future that seems the globalist powers that be, have pre planned quite some time ago with our continuing manufactured consent? I mean, what is the point of self-realization if our Physical world is destroyed or falls into a dystopia, right!? (not a loaded question, as all the above have been already suggested and pushed, in the open, shamelessly)

Ray: The point here is simply that life itself will always win and with this, the destructive, dark forces must fall. These are the wars of the Asuras, the kings of the material world, against the Suras, the Forces of Light. In the end, the Asuras are always defeated. Mankind or creation or this planet cannot die. Like all evil political movements with their dictators have fallen, they will do it in the future. It is an eternal principle that the Light is born from Darkness. But certainly, the earlier we understand what is going on and the earlier we become masters, the better it is.

SOFB Community: Notes-keeping and your preferred, suitable, and even any issues, as far as Memory techniques for, archiving, structuring, categorizing: our vast experiences, associations, analogies, etc. Some build: astral temples, rituals, theatre plays, memory palace, mind-maps, what works best for you, since you have already written dozens of books, and articles?

Ray: I keep everything very simple. My approach is to understand how things work and then I do not need to check any notes or books, etc. but things just flow into my mind. We can say that I have a good connection to Akasha, and so ideas or information are well accessible for me. Besides this, memory techniques are certainly useful to train imagination, etc.

SOFB Community: How to respond, or protect oneself, from a "black magician" who abuses akasha against you, so as to provoke your reaction and his forthcoming end, as the only thing hoping it will free him from his pacts with neg/demonic beings. (it's extremely rare, but still)

Ray: Black magicians often use astral beings to accomplish their goals. Black magicians and Akasha, the divine element of harmony are two poles which cannot fit together. Akasha would give salvation to the black magician, so that he would turn into a white magician. Akasha purifies, heals and balances everything in a merciless way. Darkness cannot survive in it. Normally it is enough to ignore a black magician. This means to not fight back. For protection, you could create a shield or a lightning conductor which conducts the energy attacks into the ground. You could also pray to the Lords of Karma for instant punishment for his evil deeds respectively you ask for justice.

SOFB Community: When long-term working, accumulating, condensing all kinds of energies (from vital to more macro-cosmic) in/through the body, or dynamic pore-breathing exercises (in bones, etc.) tend to leave one feeling tensed up, or wired, even when pore-breathing all energies out, maybe because of the cosmic nature of many energies, to get acclimated to. Any suggestions of any kind of practices, to fully dissolve all sorts of leftover tensions and opening up the body, tendons, ligaments, so as to be opened and strong conduits, but to end up feeling energized, instead of wired, like with the dynamic & aggressive breathing?

Also, any suggestions of Physical practices and training for enhancing the practices of IIH & KTQ?

Ray: Every time you accumulate any kind of universal energy in you and release it, you have caused changes in your energy system. You simply cannot feel the same like before the exercise. The main problem is that the training room can become charged easily without noticing it directly. So, this means when you feel overcharged, then it is probably the case that your room is overcharged which has strong effects on you. When you let your room exhale, releasing the extra energies, you probably feel instantly better or "normal". So, this would be the first thing which I do if I feel permanently overcharged. Besides this, "jumping into a cool swimming pool" brings direct relief as the extra energies are transferred into the water. If you have no swimming pool available, then you can put your feet into a tank with cool water and let the extra energies flow into it by will/imagination. And besides this, you can and should balance the energies in you with their opposite force to maintain balance and wellbeing. The earth element for grounding, strengthening and stabilizing is very nice and useful. We suffer in main from the electric-fiery energies. I would try first the earth element for balancing, then normal vital energy and then carefully water element or the magnetic fluid as here it could be that the fiery energies get fresh food. In general we need to strengthen the energy body with the earth element, the electromagnetic fluid to be able to bear the higher energies. Physical training helps to balance the energies as well.

SOFB Community: How to approach teaching, or gradually initiating one's relatives (siblings, parents) without revealing them your practices and your actual spiritual beliefs. The things that come to mind atm, are maybe loading their room at night with some energies that may help their exteriorization of their mental, maybe astral body as well, when sleeping, so to at least as a start to believe that there is an after-life after all. Are there any practices or other things, to do for them so they get various initiations in their sleep, and upon waking up, it would be much easier to reveal oneself, eventually, but what do you suggest though?

Ray: Even if you have the best intentions, it is going against the free will and the individual development of your family members when you try to initiate them or raise their vibration. We can only offer knowledge or practical experiences as far as others are willing to receive. Besides this, we can pray for them in general and especially for healing, good health, divine inspiration, etc.

Initiation must be a free decision. You can pick them up individually, offering them something what they understand, food for thoughts, but not much more. I know that this is disappointing but you cannot force people. Maybe watch nice movies or documentaries about spiritual topics and things like life after death, near-death-experiences and various psi-phenomena. It is easy and you can discuss things afterwards. Or go with them to special, spiritual places where they can feel the spiritual power and atmosphere. Guiding them gently to new experiences can be useful.

SOFB Community: Nibbana – Do any spirits of any of the spheres teach such subjects, or can briefly give a small taste of such an experience, since it must have come to their attention that many incarnated people from physical planet Earth attaining Nibbana (complete liberation from the cycle of reincarnation), and if yes, is it possible that such spirits knows and give a taste about it?

Ray: Nibbana or Moksha or however you want to call it is not that special. It is a state of enlightenment, of conscious freedom to do what you feel is right and in main it is about feeling no desires to incarnate again. There is nothing left for you to do or to experience in the material world, no bonds, no karma to balance, no interests, just freedom, peace, happiness, the state of perfection, completeness. So, you are free to do whatever you want respectively to follow the call for spiritual missions or to go and stay in the highest realms as an enlightened, self-realized being. Practically speaking, most return to teach or to fulfill other missions here on earth or in higher realms.

It is just the normal path of purification, training, refinement and accomplishment. There is no special initiation needed. You can find deities in the mercury sphere and in the sun sphere which are in charge of enlightenment. I have met the main deity in the sun sphere which offers all enlightenments in all various traditions on earth. Enlightenment is enlightenment, all in control of one main deity and initiator.

SOFB Community: Can one be taught by spirits, or other ways, to sense any signs, "disturbances in the force", negative or demonic entities gathering, sulphur or burnt flesh psychic smells, which-ever else, in the close environment that could mean a negative, destructive incident is going to happen soon somewhere there nearby, maybe of a terrorist or any other deadly attack. What to do besides leaving that place, environment asap, how can one react, protect, manage such situations, while leaving?

Ray: It is in general useful to get out of the resonance with such events by undergoing purification, healing and refinement. Further on, you can regularly pray for divine inspiration, guidance and protection. Then you will receive warnings. You can also create elementals which can warn you. Besides all, your intuition will let you feel that something is wrong and then you can escape. Warnings can come in many ways. Those who have eyes to see and ears to listen.....

SOFB Community: Because of mistake, re-scheduling, not knowing better, which-ever, How to cancel or neutralize an electro-magnetic volt, or other quantities, that we magically sent in akasha, with a specific purpose ?

Ray: You can create a corresponding volt or energy or elemental to cancel the first volt/energy if necessary.

SOFB Community: Bardon only mentions 24 Original beings of the EZ, And some appear to be an embodiment of their version of the whole earth zone. What is the role of the Originals, in comparison to the rest of the zodiac signs, and are there other Constellations beings and degrees, besides the usual 12 ones, and if yes, are their effects on us and the planes we are connected the same like the 12 ones?

Ray: In general, it is useful to differentiate between normal astrology and Bardon's teachings. You can contact the deity which teaches astrology to get answers or to receive a high-quality initiation into astrology. In PME Bardon talks only about the most important spirits, so there are a lot more, great hierarchies of deities, astral beings, spirits of nature, etc.

SOFB Community: How to cultivate: unshakable conviction, and faith, in our minds correctly, and that to reflect back onto the results?

Ray: It starts on a human level but really effective it becomes only when you have increased your level of personal power, of will, of authority and of belief. A master is a power plant with the divine levels of will, authority, faith, etc. However, already on the human level it makes a lot of sense to believe in yourself and to build up a strong will. If you question and doubt yourself, how should anything work out? Self-confidence and strength are the keys for success, for the successful realization of your wishes.

SOFB Community: How can those people (maybe related somehow to the water elementals of nature) who were born with a nearly superhuman level of empathy, watery root chakra, and very refreshing, alluring and magnetic life-force auric and astral fields, can protect, shield, hide, themselves in their everyday life, from normal people of all genders who not knowing any better end up stalking them due to the "high fix" they get by being near them?

What people of both physical genders who were born with the above "configurations", and especially with a rare both watery: root & sacral chakras, that have very unusual high sex drives and sexual impulses can do ? (besides their usual burning it off on sex, and other such activities)

Ray: I know this problem from female friends which are so magnetic and watery and over sensitive that they are like sponges which attract all thought, emotions and bad energies from other people and their surroundings. This is very bad. The fire element needs to be developed to balance this too strong watery pole. Further on, the earth element needs to be strengthened to stabilize the personality and the whole microcosm. A strong, dense microcosm can no longer absorb all the various energies from people and surroundings. Here it can help already to wear bracelets made of (black tourmaline) crystals. They unfold a very nice densifying, grounding, strengthening, stabilizing and protecting effect on the person. Bracelets can be used at the ankles of the feet or / and at the hands. The crystals can be programmed to unfold a cleaning as well as strengthening and vitalizing effect. In general, the person needs to work on its element balance. More air, more fire and more earth element. If the person is polluted, then a bath with 1-2 kilos of sea salt is very useful for purification and vitalization.

SOFB Community: Some hints on what needs to be done for remote healings from afar, and condensing the energies as dense as possible at the patient to an astral level I'm assuming, so as to have good healing results?

Ray: You can condense energies by normal accumulation breathing. It is already very good if you charge the patient with light several times, programming the light to support all healing processes. You can charge additionally with vital energy. Besides this, there are many possibilities to offer healing treatments.

SOFB Community: Related to Bardon's way of astral separation and travel, pro-vided one has a very strong will-power to make the necessary effort and therefore succeeds everytime, are there any ways or practices, to make it more friendly and easier to the practitioner, or will just have to get used to the unpleasant feelings of the whole procedure and when re-inhabiting the physical body upon return?

Ray: You can support all traveling exercises with the use of Akasha or / and the air element. These energies help to make the bodies go loose. Then you can work easier with your will power or further techniques.

SOFB Community: Working with the letters and the planetary energies is com-pletely exhausting particularly in the beginning. Particularly with akasha. Be-sides consistent training and adaptation, is there anything else to help offset, or recover faster?

Ray: You can balance the work with higher energies by charging yourself from time to time with normal vital energy and also with the earth element which will strengthen your energy body and structure. We must make the energy body so strong that it can manage the higher tension of the powerful energies. Besides this, I just recommend discharging from time to time your training room.

SOFB: Thank you Ray.

Ray: Thank you for the interview and all the questions!

In love, light and service, Ray del Sole.

SIFU MARK RASMUS

Introduction to Sifu Mark Rasmus

Sifu Mark Rasmus began his martial arts training in the 1970s and by 1986, he opened his first school in Brisbane, Australia under the encouragement of his Wing Chun teacher, John Dugan. After teaching his first class, Mark realized that this was his life's path and he also began his journey in Tai Chi Chuan. During the late 1970s, Mark embarked on his journey into Hermetics, when he met his first mentor, William Cook Edwards. Over the course of more than three decades, Mark has combined his expertise in martial arts and Hermetics to create the Elastic Force System, and has become a living master of Applied Hermeticism. Mark has taught thousands of students, teachers, and masters around the world the theory and application of internal martial arts, Tai Chi, Chi Kung, Hermetics, Evocation, and Quabbalah. His vision is to create masters and teachers in every discipline and area of expertise with the goal of raising the group consciousness and having an overall evolutionary impact.

Interview

SOFB Community: Dietary energetics, how to use diet to impact our training?

Sifu Mark Rasmus: Okay, so when you're working with energy, living food is the best and if you put you food under a microscope and it's alive, you're going to get a vital energy boost from it of some type. When food is more highly cooked, the life force in the food disappears, so that's the first thing to look at.

The second thing is your body type, what has an energetic resonance with you. So let's say green juice, kale juice, within one minute of a person drinking a glass of kale juice, thank you. Within one minute of a person drinking a glass of kale juice, their energy field will start to glow and it'll go from about one to two inch radiance up to four, six inch radiance. That's a substantial amplification. I haven't really checked how long that lasts for, but it's definitely noticeable and this happens with several different green juices. Having a green juice before Qigong practice, it's definitely going to work.

Traditionally you fast during meditative practice, so if you're into the keto diet, when you fast your body goes into ketosis, this will give you those benefits. The way to balance your diet out is to not eat in the morning until you've done your morning practice. Some people use one meal a day to keep themselves in ketosis and you have that meal at the end of the day, so you get all your practice beforehand and then that fixes that problem. You stay in keto, the mind is really relatively quiet because of that. Carbohydrates tend to create a lot more static in your mind than ketogenic foods, so that's something to consider.

In regards to static, when you eat meat, you want to bless the food when you eat it, connect to the akasha and the light of the spirit of the animal that it came from and do a blessing on the animal.

That will neutralize that static that comes from eating meat. If you're eating refined foods, sugary type foods, it's basically going to make a rhythmic whiplash in your field and your meditation is not going to be very high quality. When you're eating more raw foods, despite the high carbohydrate, the life force that it generates will balance that out. You have to look at are you insulin sensitive or insulin resistant within your body type. If you have any insulin resistance, which most people eat a lot of processed foods, you're better off on a ketogenic diet. If you're insulin sensitive, you'd be best off on a raw, whole food, plant-based diet. You've got to look at which is better for your body type and your health and your system as diet energetics.

SOFB Community: How to train Bardon's clairvoyance exercises, the expectations of the results, how do we ensure we are really seeing or sensing something?

Sifu Mark Rasmus: Well, you're seeing, you're not seeing. That's pretty obvious. You're feeling, you're not feeling.

You're sensing, you're not sensing. When I worked in Tarot, I had a couple of Tarot shops.

You'd start off going into the past of the person's story and then you go into the present of the person's situation and then you follow that causal stream into the future. The person you're doing the reading for gets a clear, yep, the past was correct. The present is correct. It's predictable the future will be correct as well in the reading. You're putting in some safety measures into how you do the reading. You don't just go straight to the future.

You want to create confidence that, yes, I'm on track in the causal chain of what I'm reading from the past, present and the future so you can see whether the results are real or not.

Okay. Now, we've got how to develop clairvoyance. All right, so clairvoyance, you have a causal chain. Each of the six gates of the mind first need to be separated from the intending mind and the observing mind. With our consciousness, you do the same. For example, on mental training, we observe the rising and falling wave thoughts but with your eyes open, taking in visual information.

You have the part of the mind which observes, you have the part of the mind that has intention inside of you that does and then you have the field of consciousness and information flowing. Now, you obviously want to do this with your eyes closed, watching your thoughts rise and fall away. When you're in that state where the thoughts and the mind's substance generate distance between each other, from there then you open your eyes and go into eye consciousness and observe your thoughts arise and fall away with your eyes open.

There'll be a natural tendency to, oh, that's brick, that's this, that's that, whatever you're looking at and go through the labelling process so you have to detach the labelling process because when you're in a psychic stream of information, the moment your intellect switches on and starts categorizing, labelling and organizing the information, you break the stream. People with a very contracted mental space will do more of that than people with an open space.

People with open mental space tend to be more psychic. You observe the rising and falling wave thoughts with your eyes open, observe the stream, separate the intending mind from the observing mind and then you, from there you work into, from observing to intending.

So you look at an object, you put your mind intent on the object and you observe yourself concentrate on that object visually. So what this does is the observer creates distance between the intention of observing. So you get the intending mind extending out and holding the state that you're in and the observing mind sits in the background and looks at the bigger picture.

So you have a small picture and a big picture simultaneously in your sensory system. From there, both of these two exercises are going to create an accumulation of emptiness underneath your consciousness. So when you watch your thoughts arise and fall away, the thoughts get further and further from you and everything starts to become still, so like your mental space becomes buffered with stillness. That's the accumulation of akasha.

Any form of concentration will accumulate akasha, but not all types of akasha are the same. If you're doing a vipassana based observing, rising, falling wave, the akashic substance is very soft. If you're doing a samahadhi, high concentration type of exercise, one pointed and occupying a smaller space, the akasha accumulation is much sharper and glossy and clearer and it's like a sword, it's a different type of akasha.

The meditation object you use affects the nature of the akasha that accumulates underneath the object and underneath your mind as you concentrate. So you want to do eye concentration with big space and eye concentration with small space to accumulate these two different types of emptiness. Then you make emptiness your meditation object. You sit in equanimity in your eye consciousness. From there we move on to vital breathing through the eyes, so you tune into the feeling of life force, you feel with your eyes, breathe life force in, life force out, and you get that from the building of the ball, qigong set.

Once you've done that vital breathing through the eyes, then you do the balancing your elements in the four regions. Vital breathe, release time, slow everything down into the astral fluid, then tune to the earth element, breathe the earth into the legs, and meditate on equanimity. Water into the water region, air into the air, fire into the fire. And then what I want you to do is once you've contemplated that feeling of equanimity and stillness in each one of those areas, go into your solar plexus, collapse into that stillness and make your mind smaller and smaller like you're sinking inwards. And there's a particular type of vacuity that you're going to get. And then take that out of your solar plexus and touch your earth region and touch the stillness. Just make your whole earth element still through your body. And it's just like you're just going touch, boom, and then you have an overwhelming astral quietude in your earth.

Then touch your water region with it, touch your air, touch your fire, and then go back into your solar plexus and you'll be able to collapse into a deeper stillness and cycle through this. So you learn how to touch the elemental regions of your body with your mind with a vacuous stillness to amplify deeper equanimity within each element, which gives you deeper access to the infinity quality in your solar plexus. Okay, once you've done that, you take that infinity quality from the solar plexus and you put it in eye consciousness. You breathe it through the eyes in and out. And what this does is it separates the layers of consciousness of your eyes. When you have any emotional relationship to something you see, you get a stickiness between your mental, astral, and physical body, and you need to equalize that stickiness.

So you're separating the layers of eye consciousness. In doing so, you'll quickly realize that you have the organ of the eyes, you have the consciousness of the eyes, you have information flowing into the consciousness of the eyes, and then you have the consciousness from where that information comes. So everything in the universe is mind.

The wall in front of me is mind substance. That mind substance is reflecting light and it mixes, the mind substance mixes with that light to come through with information to reach my eye consciousness and the organ of the body receives it. So I want to separate those layers and the reason why is at the end, it's all mind substance. My mind substance through the organ, through the consciousness, through the information of the mind substance of what I'm looking at interacts and you pull the layers apart and you have clairvoyant experiences.

When the layers collapse back into each other, the clairvoyant stops. So the akasha neutralizes the mental astral matrix of those layers and just opens everything up and that opens your clairvoyance when you're in eye consciousness and you're doing that. So from there to amplify that, you invoke light.

Now you can do the method of pore breathing the akasha, looking at your mind, your mind essentially is light. There'll be a personified mind of like a star type quality that is the center of gravity of your own mind and then there's a field that star vibrates on which is more of a universal divine light. So one has a personified identity to it and then the other is a field oneness identity to it and as you move through that, you can invoke light and breathe it in and out of the eyes with a prayer to invoke clairvoyance.

As you invoke that clairvoyance, you're going to be generating a self-fulfilling prophecy inside prayer in akasha and inviting that in. If that prayer has a very altruistic quality to it, you're going to find that it will function for the benefit of others. We're built for evolution.

Everything is constantly evolving and we're evolving for the next generation. So if you use a motive that you're awakening clairvoyance for the benefit of others, then the information that you're going to receive clairvoyantly and the service you're going to provide towards the evolution of the group consciousness that pulls through you because it's released of time and it amplifies your clairvoyance. You're part of a bigger evolutionary field of consciousness and you're in service to that evolution, so the power and energy flowing through you is amplified dramatically. So put a seed inside the prayer that's for the benefit of others.

The next thing you want to do is have a look at how you pray. There's a vibrational scale inside that. You have a frequency of humility, you have a frequency of devotion to your spiritual path, you have a frequency of reverence, you have a frequency of sacredness and this generates a type of akasha in the prayer. So when we looked at your meditation objects and how different styles of meditation accumulate different types of akasha, when your meditation object is a vibrational scale of prayer, of the humility of the prayer, the devotion of the prayer, the reverence of the prayer, the sacredness of the prayer and akasha is invoked through the prayer, that generates a different type of akasha.

It's more in resonance with an infinite, unlimited akasha than a limited type of akasha.

When you have that non-self ideal inside your valve, how and why you're training it, if it's for the next generation, there's a continuity of consciousness in the function of what you're invoking through the prayer which continues out, which relates to that infinity, which increases success within the prayer to invoke clairvoyance for the benefit of others.

So look at the metaphysical framework of how and why you're training a clairvoyance and what its functions are. So when you invoke that light in prayer through the akasha and you're invoking the frequency of clairvoyance through the prayer, you invite that down through the crown or through the pores and you fill the eyes with it and then you get your body to equalize with that.

Now the type of clairvoyance you're working with will be unique to each person and its function, what is a clairvoyance for? If you're a healer and you want to investigate disease, okay, then that's a specific type of clairvoyance. You want to look right into the cells, right into the physiology, right into the chemistry.

If you're a counsellor and you don't see the past, present, future alignment of how the person's feeling, thinking in action and where they've been and where they're going then how you can counsel them to make better decisions and things to release within their perception and reality so they can have a better quality of life, different type of clairvoyance. You need to look at what type of clairvoyance you want to invoke.

SOFB Community: Okay the next thing is accumulating the four elements more effectively and how to deepen stillness in the mind.

Sifu Mark Rasmus: Okay to accumulate the elements more effectively you need to release time before you astrally breathe. So when you breathe, I teach a four cycle breath to beginners. You draw the life force in through the pores which you learnt from building the ball. You pause and stop the mind. When you stop the mind and the breath, everything stands still so you go into that stillness and then you breathe the stillness through the life force slowing everything down and then you pause at the other end of the breath and breathe the stillness so you're circulating the stillness in and out through your field of consciousness and everything gets slower and slower. The energy thickens. Once you've got to that thick, heavy space, then swing the energy towards the element.

Then start breathing the qualities of water so you water the body mechanics, giving yourself a hug. You pull the joints open. Water element has and the fascial web has a different type of mechanic to fire. Fire the joints are expanding, water the joints are pulling. If you pick up a baby and give the baby a hug, there's a protective aspect to it. There's a holding, nurturing, it's a part of your field. It's like your drop of water and the baby's drop of water unify and then becomes one drop of water. That's the water element.

Everything has cohesion and draws in as a pulling aspect to it. You look at what are the qualities of the water element you're tuning into. What's the information? What are the body mechanics and what does my mind concentrate on when you do that? From that astral fluid, which you develop by releasing time on life force, it's electromagnetic and you swing towards the magnetic, then you swing towards the electric. Once you have these two basic poles separated, you raise up and stretch everything up through your fascia to the air and then you relax and connect to gravity and synchronize with gravity for the earth.

That astral fluid will flux between the basic quadrapolar magnet qualities. Once you've done that, you place them in the four regions, do the collapsing, which we just talked about earlier, into the solar plexus, touch each region with stillness and go back into the sole plexus and circulate through that exercise getting deeper and deeper. If you're applying the kabalistic sounds, the sh, the a, the m, and the ae into the legs, that's the incorrect pronunciation, and you just go through that four little formula when you start, you equalize the static in your body and the elements and go into equanimity straight away. You just touch each of those areas with a letter and you drop into equanimity. That equanimity, you'll swing that towards whichever gate of the mind you're working on in your development. Okay, so accumulating the elements is basically get good at astral breathing first and then work with the elements and don't go overboard. You only use as much heat in your body as what you'd use if you got angry to regulate the fire element to bring your body into equanimity. It's about generating equanimity, not about generating fire element. It's how much do you need for equanimity of the fire, and that applies to all the elements.

SOFB Community: How to safely look into or receive in this current life any past life skills, abilities we had back then, but without activating or receiving any negative karma related to each of those skills, abilities, or powers in those former lives?

Sifu Mark Rasmus: Okay, so to invoke past life skills, you have to first be very good at working in akasha and moving down that akasha timeline with your mental body, so there's a type of timeline training where you slide backwards.

Past life skills are like mountain peaks, you know, you'll jump from mountain peak to mountain peak, and those peaks are peak skills that are in resonance with this incarnation.

It's very, very difficult to disconnect the karma of generating a skill from the skill and because of the causal chain that allowed you to generate it astrally in that incarnation. So if we, let's say, look at a samurai who spent his whole life concentrating swinging a sword, and he generated extreme samahadhi every time he picks up the sword, and that samahadhi expresses through his astral body, through his spirit, and his spirit aligns and he's got that concentration and is deeply grounded in the sword. As he starts to move through akasha and touch non-dual light, the non-dual light arises through those physiological state, that astral state, that mental state, the patterning of concentration that's in resonance with the sword. Now, when he tries to invoke light without his sword, it'll be very difficult, and there's a physical aspect to it, there's an astral aspect to it, there's a mental, there's akashic and there's a non-dual aspect to it. And this causal chain of interaction restricts how he can teach this light he's connected to.

So when he invokes the spirit and invokes light, in order for him to share the gains of his life's work with someone else, he needs to pick up a sword. He has to pick that sword up, teach the technique of the sword, use the vehicle of the sword, the astral nature of the sword, the mental nature of the sword, the akashic nature, the non-dual light nature, and a causal chain is via the sword. He can't go, okay, I'm just going to do some healing on you with non-dual light now, because the bridges weren't built that way. And his skill has a causal chain that's dependent on that skill. So when you go into any particular past life skill, you need to build your physical framework in resonance with that particular skill from that past life, you need to build your astral framework in resonance with that skill in that life, you need to build your mental framework in resonance with that skill in that past life, go into the akashic and invoke it and let it pass through your mental, astral, physical body so it can be expressed in that way.

So you can already see that there's some problems there. You're going to be invoking a lot of karma from those past lives, you're going to be invoking a lot of memories, feelings, emotions, physiological states, because they're associated with the causal chain. To filter them out, the only way that I've found I can do that, and I don't get the same peak results as I did in those incarnations, but what I do is I get the insight of how it works, and how to develop it, and how to move into a formless state and back to forms that's more relative to this incarnation, and that is, it's a flux between non-dual light and akasha. You go through the akasha, you touch the incarnation, and then you relax into the non-dual light of that incarnation, the non-dual state of that skill, and you invite that down through your crown, through your three bodies, and it will generate a new alignment to how that skill could work within this incarnation, within how your mental, astral, and physical body is aligned, and what exercises and activities you need to allow that skill to present itself in this incarnation.

Because it's brought from the non-dual light state down, you're not drawing the karma with it, you're just drawing the information inside the skill, but the skill isn't ripe, it's not magic, it's not, you can just do something, you understand how to do it, but you still have to do the hard work of building the frame mentally, astral, and physically, because you always need the three bodies to do any type of magic.

SOFB Community: From a hermetic perspective, what further information or insights can be gained regarding the stages of spiritual attainment such as stream entry, once return, non-return, and the experiences or realms that individuals may encounter after death according to Hermetic teachings?

Sifu Mark Rasmus: Okay, so, a stream intro is someone who's achieved basic samahadhi, so when you practice increasing concentration, you reach this point in your concentration where, how do we say this, where there's a critical mass, where you can watch yourself concentrate, you have a focused mind, you can step away from yourself and go, oh, I'm still concentrating, that the observing mind, the concentrating mind, the layers start pulling apart, and there's critical mass inside the layers, and you can watch yourself practice without interrupting your practice, this is stream entry.

The once returner is where that gets deep enough into the spirit to generate a karmic stickiness in the light of your spirit that will magnetically pull you back into the alignment on your next incarnation to be on the Buddhist path, to be on the path of light, and that you have enough magnetic pull there to ensure that is the case.

A non-returner is a person who's achieved non-dual life, and there's a lot of people who, in a past incarnation, they were a monk, they had a very good samahadhi skill, they achieved non-dual light, and when they passed away, their spirit raised up into the non-dual light state, the divine light, and when they, entered that state, they had a freedom of choice, do they want to reincarnate again or not, and the stickiness on their mental body is less than their center of gravity of connection to their samahadhi and light.

That's because this critical mass of concentrating on light, and you can observe that without your mind being pulled in, there's a point at which, when you leave the body, you stick to that light, and you can observe it, and there's not enough samsaric force to force another incarnation, so you're a non-returner, you can sit with a non-dual light if you choose.

It's not true non-dual light because there's a small amount of flux for you to move and develop yourself, if it's truly non-dual, you couldn't move towards nirvana, where in these states you can move towards nirvana, but very slowly. One year on earth, 500 years on heaven is functioning, and that one year development here is 500 years development there, there's a big difference, so beings who are in this state realize very quickly the law of rhythm on earth has this spectrum, the rhythmic movement is tiny in that space, and the time continuum differences, they all want to reincarnate and go back into the path of service and evolve themselves.

Okay, so the center of gravity of your mental body, if you're a biker, you like drinking smoking and indulging in biker-type activities, as soon as your physical body dies, is in resonance with biker heaven, that's where you're going to go, you're going to end up in that space. And your mental body will like all the tractor-like and you'll come to like resonance of the centre of gravity of your spirit, whatever state of static and vibration that is, or absence of static.

So if you were doing an akashic sit and you're deep in akashic trance and something happened to your physical body, and you disconnected, you'd be lost in akasha, because your mental body would have a certain critical mass in that moment in akasha, and there's many spirits lost in akasha, in the same way there's many spirits who are ghosts who have a traumatic death, and the trauma of their death makes physical and astral substance stick to their mental body, so that the center of gravity of the mental body can't move into normal reincarnation process, because they have too much traumatic astral substance stuck to them, so they become ghosts.

So when you encounter ghosts, these ghosts are very closely stuck to the physical world because of that astral substance, and the first thing you do is surround them with akasha and dissolve the stickiness, then you go to the light of their spirit and you do three transformations raising them up into light, and the moment you do this, they're freed of that astral hold that's holding them as a ghost, and they get freed up. And when they get freed up, their spirit rises and they can go into the normal reincarnation process again.

So it's trauma that sticks to the spirit that stops the normal system from functioning how it should function.

SOFB Community: In various traditions around the world, there are mentions of individuals who are believed to have achieved physical immortality, such as Mahum, Tata, and others. What insights can be gained from these traditions regarding the attainment of physical immortality? Are there possibilities for individuals to combine worldly powers, longevity, and the pursuit of nirvana while living in the physical world? Additionally, what are the purposes and goals of these immortal beings, and is it possible for them to eventually choose to break their immortality and pursue nirvana after an extended period of time?

Sifu Mark Rasmus: No, they can't. And the reason why they can't is because if someone is on the path of nirvana, it's a totally different path to the path of longevity. It's a different path to the path of worldly powers.

When you're looking for worldly power, you're bringing things into form, so the energy is coming down, mental, astral, physical, and you're interacting with the akasha to produce things in form. You're creating an infrastructure of magic. When you're working, developing nirvana, you're bringing things out of form. You're deconstructing the fabric of your astral nature, you're deconstructing your system and going into a formless state. Those of you who have met an arahant, it's like you can see straight through them. There's a part of them which is emptied of intent, and it's sort of like, wow, they're almost transparent in their energy field.

They're very clear, and we're not talking about clear light. This is someone who's on that non-dual light level. We're talking about the energetic framework of doing so much akasha and non-dual light work that all the stickiness, mentally, astrally, and physically is released. Now, just doing this to the mental body will allow a person to touch the nirvana, but they'll have an astral mess there, so they might be still addicted to cigarettes, and like many arahants in Thailand that are chain smokers, their physical astral body is a mess.

They don't train any mortality, they don't care about their body, they only care when they enter into meditation that they go through this process of releasing. These guys, they're touching nirvana, but they're doing it in a very different way to someone who's leading a pure path, who's got, let's say, a tai chi body, and they released all the tension in their body, they've cleaned up their astral body, and they've cleaned their mental body, and they're radiating light through all the bodies, then they enter nirvana.

They produce a different type of thing to the arahants in Thailand who kind of have the outward persona of a chain smoking bum. Different thing. Now, you'll quickly realize once you've met some of these people about their astral nature, okay, I was in a temple, and I met a monk, and we started chatting, and he seemed like a very chatty type of character and very flamboyant, so I'm going, oh, okay, he's very bright, and then he said, oh, I just have to finish this ritual, and he made a prayer, and the whole space went quiet around where we were standing, and he invoked a type of acuity, so his mental power was totally different to an astral personality.

They were chalk and cheese, and if he hadn't presented that prayer, I may have missed his spiritual power because I just wasn't looking for it, but when he made that prayer, lit the incense, did the blessing, and then the whole space went into the akasha around him, it's like, wow, this guy's got some skills, so the mental body skill and power and the astral body contaminants and the physical body, they're three separate bodies. Buddhists who are working towards nirvana, especially in the Theravada system, they're only concerned with their mental body. They trash their astral and physical bodies, it's kind of a strange phenomenon, but it's there.

Immortals, in the Himalayas, ever since as a child, there's like a magnet pulling my spirit to the Himalayas, and in the caves, there's hermits living there that I don't know how old they are, but they're radiating such intense light that I've felt them ever since I was about six, seven years old. It's been a pull, and at that age, I didn't know what that pull was, and as I got older and looked at a map, I went, something's pulling me to that place, and these spiritually highly developed people are extremely closed off. They don't interact with the world. Socially developed people tend to be introverted, tend to not like to associate with people. They tend to hide themselves, and they don't want anyone to know their path.

In Franz Bardon's work, he says, don't tell anyone about what you do. Be very, very secretive. You put that on steroids, and you have these people who are striving towards immortality.

They're extremely quiet. Now, some people say, oh, Mark, why are you sharing all this information? If you were a real practitioner, you'd be really quiet about it, and you wouldn't put any videos on the internet, and there's a certain degree of truth in that, in that when I post a lot of information on the internet, there's a draw of energy from me. There's a drain.

It's like people are sticking hooks into my energy field and draining and drawing energy off me. What I need to do to post information, share information on how to develop yourself in hermetics remain more detached from the internet and from people and from those videos. When I record videos like this, I don't even watch them. I'll just trim the front and back off for when I start the video and finish the video and then upload. I don't look at them. I don't really connect to them, and I disconnect, and I feel all the energy coming in, and I just neutralize it with akasha and ignore it so that it doesn't pull me down.

Now, if you look at a yogi in India who did some video footage and interviews when he was young, he's radiating light, really altruistic, and like, wow, this person's got it but 20, 30 years later, they've allowed themselves to become too much in the public eye, they've got a big following, the energy's all dirty, they've got all these weird sexual problems floating around their energy field, and they've lost it.

Very often, it's not that they're going, I'm chasing money, I'm doing this, I'm doing that. Some of them are, but the more they try and help people, the more people's hooks get into them, and you put a thousand people around you with the hooks in, they pull you down. You can't sit in that non-dual light and totally transcend the physical, astral, mental path of service. The path of service means you've got to jump into the sewer to clean people, and that's the case in India. It's got that vibe.

They'll come down to these really heavy, astrophysical environments and be in service, so they're going to get dirty, and if they're not careful, they get caught in the projections of the culture onto the yogi, onto the master, and they lose it. If they get too many anchors pulled in, they get pulled down. Practices need to remain very detached from the knowledge they share and the people they connect to so that they don't get pulled down. You have to do regular cleanup as a teacher where you just demagnetize your mental, emotional, physical relationship to people so you don't get too caught.

Having said that, the Buddha said, your friends are your path. He didn't say it's a part of the path, he said it's the path you walk on. Think about that. You take your three closest friends, add them together, divide by three, and you look in the mirror and say, oh, that's a big part of me. You're astro-unconscious patterning how you think, feel, and act in your yearnings are

a reflection of those people. When you're going through this spiritual development process, you quickly realize the people you trust, the people you confide in, they have a very strong unconscious regulation of your energy patterns, and that is your spiritual path. That's your map. That's what you're walking on. Pick your friends very, very, very wisely.

Let's continue on this.

SOFB Community: Is it possible to attain nirvana without a spiritual community? How can one avoid getting entangled in societal attachments and distortions? Can an arahant and their sangha be the key to achieving this?

Sifu Mark Rasmus: My teacher had achieved nirvana, and he pulled the entire class in nirvana one day and said, okay, pulled everyone up, everyone touched it, and once that taste was there, I could never forget that taste. So I could take that taste and put it in the equanimity underlying these layers, and even though I never went back into full nirvana because I chose to be married and chose to be in public life and have this fabricated reality that I'm in, the flavor never left me.

It's a yearning that's always there, and because of that direct experience, there's always when the spirit goes into equanimity, the magnetic pull towards it increases. So as I age and I get to this place in my life where, okay, I'm semi-retiring, I'm reducing my teaching load, I can start taking more time and retreat myself to touch nirvana and re-enter that state that my teacher was nice enough to give me, then I can take ownership of it.

Now, if he hadn't given me that experience in 1988, I don't know whether I would be able to go back there on my own accord, to be able to just access that through releasing and using conventional Buddhist methods. It would be extremely difficult, where if you're around someone who has touched nirvana and they leave that flavor inside you, and that flavor is a knowing of exactly how to re-access it, then you can go and do that practice and you can re-access it.

But unless you have achieved nirvana in a past life and are waiting to re-awaken and re-achieve it in this incarnation, very, very unlikely. If nirvana's your goal, find someone who's touched nirvana, and not someone like myself who's touched nirvana, though haven't taken ownership of it yet. I may, as I get older and have more time for this, have to just sit in equanimity for 12 hours a day and be sensitive to those high layers of light and releasing my attachment to those lights, I'm highly addicted to light.

I've been reincarnating in a non-dual light in the sun for a lot of incarnations, and it's highly addictive, because everything you need spiritually nurtures you inside that light. It's full and complete. So why would I want to leave that? So I have a lot of work to do to release my connection to the sun and release my connection to path of service to dissolve all those things, go long or go further. I was very fortunate that I had someone implant that path inside me, that if I choose that, it's there.

So find an Arahant who's already taken ownership, take 10 years of your life to follow the Arahant, and if you're 100% committed, I'm sure you can achieve nibbana. And it's very achievable. After I had that experience with my teacher and the clarity of that, everything you do is an exercise for touching equanimity, everything. And if you recognize you touch the elements in your body with equanimity, you touch your mind with equanimity, and equanimity is the elevator, the door to all things, all spiritual levels that exist, including nibbana, that you are just cultivating an equanimous relationship between your mind, equanimity and object, then nibbana becomes, it's very, very doable. It's something that's open to everybody, as long as they understand that equanimity is the door. And all practice produces equanimity, which allows the mind to work up and down the vibrational scale and make ascension a part of your reality.

Okay, let's move forward. So yes, you don't need monastic life, but you do need to have the company of an Arahant who's attained nirvana to achieve that.

SOFB Community: I would like a suggestion on how to do the visualization exercises.

Sifu Mark Rasmus: Okay, so I had a student who had been doing visualization exercise for a couple of years and failed. And he was going through an initiation text, but he wasn't communicating with me. I didn't know where he was at. And he said, 'I'm going to give up, I can't do this anymore'.

And so I looked at him and said, okay, can you visualize your girlfriend's tits? Anyway, he said 'of course', I said, what's the problem? And he called me up the next day and said, yep, I've mastered visualization. Now in Buddhism, that would be an incorrect method because it's such a strong attachment, but it gave him the understanding that the magnetic fluid in the metal astral matrix that binds you to a visual object is the key or door to mastering visualization. So if you charge vitally, astrally, mentally a visual object, you'll be able to hold it in your mind really clearly. So for me, when my daughter was born, it was a very intense moment. And that visual is super clear.

Now the same mental astral cohesion I had to that, I can put onto any visual object and visualize it clearly. And then from there, I transfer my mental body to the visual object and identify I am the vision. I can demagnetize the mental and astral, so I don't need my physical body. I don't need my astral body. I tune in and identify I am this, so then I can see that. And then you can do it without the mental astral fluid to help you visualise. So it's a stepping stone to that state.

SOFB Community: Can you provide insights on the relationship between non-dual light and the dantians in the context of spiritual practices? Additionally, how do akashic exercises relate to the cultivation and integration of non-dual light?

Sifu Mark Rasmus: Okay, so when you balance the four elements, the four regions, you go into the soul plexus, you collapse your mind inwards, and it's easier to touch akasha collapsing form inwards than going outwards.

So you go inwards. And once you have that infinity quality from sinking inwards, you poor-breathe it. And you learn how to poor-breathe it into any object your mind touches, so that you can go into the infinity of the object and enter into akasha underneath things.

Once you've gone into the akasha underneath things, your mind gets this ability to look at itself from akasha, so it's kind of like a reverse mirror. And when you start doing that, first thing you notice is that your mind is this light, and your mind is sticky, and your mind is subject to an identity, and subject to wanting to be a form. So it tends to manifest itself in a star.

Sometimes those stars take on sacred geometry type patterns to reflect the frequency of the star, so underneath you'll have different types of geometry, but we won't go into that. It's a star. Now it's individualized. That light will vibrate in a field of light, and it's a star in a field of light. Now, as you observe this from akasha, your mind is going to go from identifying itself as I am the star, to I am this field of light, and that's the non-dual light, divine light. And so this stage is very important, because this is where the teachings of Buddhism come into play on non-self. And when you're working with the non-self from that field of light, then the achievement of nirvana becomes accessible, because that field of light is still fabrication.

This is where the Buddhist system opens up the last door, and has a huge amount of value in how to work on the higher levels. Now, despite what people think, Buddhism isn't a very good system for beginners, because it doesn't teach you how to develop psychic ability. You have to be highly empathic, highly psychic to understand Buddhism. It is the last door, it is the highest system on this planet.

When you read about Buddhism, it is not what the intellect will fabricate intellectually about each of the teachings of Buddhism. It is a different thing. Every tuning fork in the Dharma emanates a particular type of frequency, and you put these tuning forks together as alchemical process, spiral for ascension, and to release self. And it's the light of self that you're releasing, so it's a highly complex thing, and you need a high degree of intuitive intellect to comprehend and understand it. Reading books on Buddhism is a waste of time, really. You're better off focusing on how to develop your intuitive framework, your psychic abilities, so that you can later understand Buddhism.

SOFB Community: What about non-dual light in relation to the dantians?

Sifu Mark Rasmus: Okay, so when we're working the three centers of gravity, I teach several different models on working with light, depending on the structure of the person. The three transformations up, each dantian is the centre of gravity of the mental astral physical body. You bring both light down through the three centres, from the crown touches the mental body, it radiates light into your mental space, and it dissolves static, so your samadhi gets stronger. When you bring it into your astral body, it allows deeper equanimity of the astral elements, so you can go deeper into akasha, which generates astral samahadhi. And then when you bring it into your physical body, it reduces static in your physical body in relation to synchronicity of the three dantians, so that you can synchronise your spiritual life physically. These types of things, there's not a lot of value in talking about them, because they're just words. You need to practise non-dual light and be guided through that process to get benefit, really.

SOFB Community: I would be interested in what your take on daily introspection and the soul mirror work is.

Sifu Mark Rasmus: Okay, so every thought, feeling, and action you have during the day, you want to touch it with equanimity. So you have a mind, a static experience, mentally, astral, physically, and you touch that with equanimity and go into the empty space underneath it, and recognize it's fundamentally an illusion, and you float your mind above the illusion, and that's your daily mirror work. And you do that as a continuous self-awareness on all your experiences as you're touching your daily experiences, so you vibrate above them. This can only really be done if you've been doing astral and light work, so that you can empty out the fabrication.

You don't want to be building more fabrication in your daily life, in that you don't want to be fabricating stickiness in your mental, astral, physical body. You want to be demagnetizing and equalizing that, so that you can ascend. So yeah, you have spiritual freedom, and that becomes your daily mirror work. Any tools and means to train the fire colours and air notes, sounds, poles, and letters. I don't want to accumulate in the room any wrong, anti-genius realms, colour, or a wrong one.

SOFB Community: At what point does one realise the three sense poles are actually concentrating producing the letter vibration, you're not just wasting time combining things you don't want to match together?

Sifu Mark Rasmus: So I'm guessing you're talking about the Kabbalistic letters, and you're accumulating in the room. Okay, so go into the sun sphere, and the last of the spiritual sun sphere is the founder of Kabbalah, and you invoke him into your mental body, breathe into the sun sphere first, bring him in, and get him to pronounce the sounds, emanate the colours, and bring the frequencies of each letter through you, and you'll be doing a totally different animal to Franz Bardon's book. It gives the framework, but the colours, sounds, tones, everything's different.

It's much more akin to Tibetan deep throat singing. You know the Tibetans have this, so these very, very, very deep sounds in the sun sphere that are the source of Kabbalah are the only way to learn Kabbalah.

Learning from the book, you can't, I've never seen anyone even come close to succeeding.

You need to go to the sun sphere, go to the founder of Kabbalah, invoke that spiritual consciousness and let him take over your mental, astral, physical body, guide you through the process and learn it. I can't actually teach Kabbalah, I can only teach a person how to learn Kabbalah. You need to get to a point where you can invoke this consciousness, the essence and fabric of what Kabbalah is, and let it speak through you and receive direct transmission from the deity.

You can't get it from a person, and I've tried to, because I've been working with the sun sphere for over 30 years, and I can produce these things inside me, but when I give them to a student and produce them in the student, the student can't keep them. They'll have a blissful experience and go, wow, that was great, but it gets lost. Because the transmission needs to come directly through their intuitive framework, if I place my intuitive framework over yours and will it into you, you get it, but you didn't have the intuitive framework to pull it through you to start with, so you lose it. So all high spiritual teachings are received through deity yoga, through directly invoking it from these universal consciousness layers, and they can't, you don't need a teacher. You need a teacher for the first book, and then once you've done the first book, you are the teacher.

You're a vibrational match to God already, and you need to recognize that, and when you recognize that resonance, you bring yourself in the resonance of any cosmic frequencies you want, they pass through you and you learn. You are the teacher. You don't need me.

You don't need anyone else. Just sit quietly, you'll release time. Keep sitting quietly, you'll release space. Keep sitting quietly, you see the light of mind. You keep sitting quietly, you release fabrications of that light of mind, and if you keep sitting quietly, you attain nirvana, or touch God, whatever view you've got about it, so it's just equanimity. You have to learn to enter equanimity into each experience, touch equanimity of the experience and ascend. Okay, so that's how you tune those color sound relationships.

SOFB Community: Supposedly the gym training is utilised as a means to mostly train the will and any energies, elements, fluids. If you don't need your body to strengthen your will, then up to which point or stage can the gym training and the energy be worked on? Can one substitute the gym for any other meditation or means?

Sifu Mark Rasmus: Well, you don't need the gym. Most monks and practices walk, and for me, walking is a wonderful practice. Shugendo guys, they sort of rock up in the mountains. Gym training peaks your electric fluid out and it makes your growth leap, so you get huge, huge ramping up of energy very, very quickly. Because I teach chi kung, where people are wanting to learn power and are given the best methods for developing power, but it's not the best methods for developing nirvana or releasing. You don't need power for that, you need equanimity. So it's your mind's relationship to what you touch, to how you equalize with that relationship to ascend, to reduce the stickiness. Equanimity dissolves that stickiness. In this process, you have form Jhanas, form states, and then you have formless Jhanas and you have equanimity in the middle.

If you went to equanimity and form, you'd end up in between equanimity here and form there, you'd end up in this middle place, which is equanimity. But if you train formless akasha, which is the vacuous stuff underneath form, you equalize the form, so you end up in equanimity.

So you need formless akasha training to equalize things. If you just touch it with equanimity, you end up halfway between where you are and equanimity. Do you understand that concept? So you touch with akasha, you drop into equanimity. When you touch high levels of stress in the gym, where you're tuning your fascia with akasha, you generate an equanimity in regards to stress. So when you have normal small levels of stress, when you have small levels of stress, then you'll find that it can't touch you because you equalize such high levels of stress. Then the conductive power that moves through your facial network when you're doing energy work, that becomes obviously very evident that you can just stream 10 times more through your facial web when it's strong. Gymnastic work is probably the best balance out of all that. and climbing is one of the pinnacle exercises for facial web training and energy conduction.

SOFB Community: In the theory section of Bardon's teachings, he discusses the qualities of the spirit in relation to the elements. Could you provide further insights or commentary on these qualities?

Sifu Mark Rasmus: Okay, so earth element is omnipresence. You get this from non-dual light training where you feel connected to everything, everything is an extension, a part of you when you're in that state of frequency. And so that's a universal quality of the earth element. Now if you pick up a baby, and you hold the baby, you're magnetic, your body's in a magnetic state, you're protected, you love, you're nurturing, you encapsulate the baby, you come into a state of like a maternal oneness with the baby, you love that baby. Now if you take that as a vibrational scale through childbirth, you're working for the next stage of evolution of the group consciousness.

You're evolving, you're giving your DNA, your knowledge, everything you have to the baby for its evolution, and there's this release of time that takes place inside that. And when we look at universal love, metta, it's an understanding of this causal evolutionary curve and looking at your inner connection to everything around you, and then dedicating yourself for that benefit, it generates an insight into what universal love is. And it's evolution itself and the mechanisms that make evolution function as a unified field of universal love. So each one of these qualities can't be defined intellectually, their qualities are spirit, they're formless, so you can only make metaphors like these to describe what they are.

The air element is insight and understanding of things. When you are working with a non-dual light, and you're in the information field of how things come into form, you get an unconscious knowing of how things function. And depending on your education, you are limited by how your mind is restricted by your ability to metabolize information light into form. So I have a limited education, that means my understanding of this information, I can't translate it. I don't know how the inner function of a computer works, so I can't translate light information in relation to that. I can't go to the leading edge of IT and take it to the next level, because I don't have the education to do that. My education is limited to certain areas. Now I can look at, ah, this is what computers are going to do in the future, and the way they're going to be connected to people is going to be really, really interesting, and how small they're going to get is very, very interesting, and our connection to the world is wow, okay, you know, it's one group consciousness through computers, so it's going to be a fascinating future.

How that works, I don't know, I can't intellectualize that, I'm not a computer engineer. So when you're looking at the air element and that insight mind, it's restricted by the chemistry of your brain, the neurogenesis of your brain, how you educate yourself. So for many years, I decided three hours a day in my evenings, I'm going to study to educate myself in all these different areas so that I can make sense of all this energy coming through, and you'll find yourself becoming highly addicted to educating yourself to neurogenesis when you practise non-deal light.

These two just work together, and they'll just become a natural part of your experience. So when you're working with these types of principles, they become self-evident when you're inside of light, and omnipotence of the fire element, it's a type of divine will. It's when you express your will, and it's not the will that we look at as extreme concentration, primordial mind, or anything like that, it's much more of an interconnected sense of control of light when you're in a field of light, that you identify so much with it that your Will is able to express that divine quality through that light. So it's, again, something that can't be verbalized.

SOFB Community: How might the fundamental skills of tai chi chuan - ting, listening, and sung release - be rediscovered and incorporated into a new internal martial art in a dystopian world where all information and forms related to internal martial arts have been lost or destroyed?

Sifu Mark Rasmus: Okay, so this is a very long question. Okay, we press the delete button on internal martial arts. And when it's deleted, what's going to come back? Well, vital breathing is obviously going to come back, the facial web radiates vital energy. And as we, as we, the science develops us understand the fascia and vital energy, it will automatically begin to generate more and more methods for sports to continue on on that journey. Okay, so vital energy automatically reactivates within sports science.

Slowing energy down, slowing the mind down to vital energy will generate with an understanding of what astral energy is, it'll just happen.

When people follow common sense, push your joints open, oh, I've got more vital energy.

Now slow my mind down, oh, I've got more astral energy. Common sense will prevail and people just follow this natural rhythms, but only highly empathic people understand them.

Now, we talked about a layering process, some other videos (Mark Rasmus youtube channel), where you look at each subconscious skill when you learn to breathe vital energy as a subconscious skill, that you breathe, watch yourself breathe vital energy, a part of your personality learns to access out and use vital energy on its own independent of your own intent.

Then when we take that into the next level of going into the astral and working with astral personalities of energy, you very, very quickly find that psychologists who are working with energy will very, very quickly figure out that we have all these subconscious layers of personality that are developing independent personalities that are using energy to do things. This is why most Qigong masters can't teach their skill, they develop unconscious layers of skill that interact with each other to be able to do things, but they can't see them doing it.

So if you do a lot of vital breathing and watch yourself vital breathe and separate your intent from vital breathing, you're unconscious to learn how to control vital energy. It's unconscious in that it's a personality layer that does that. When you get these personality layers interacting and building intrinsic energies and producing different types of Fajin and you separate yourself from that awareness of how it forms, you can't teach that to another person. You have to be able to see that, ah, these layers of my own unconscious mind have developed through these years of training and I am able to do interesting stuff. If a person is not empathic enough and sensitive enough to pulling apart things into equanimity on a regular basis, they simply won't have that skill set. Okay, so last question.

SOFB Community: Anything you can say related to *Dzogchen, Trekchod,* rainbow body practices?

Sifu Mark Rasmus: In relation to this, I don't know, but I know a whole series of rainbow body practices that may or may not be the same as this. When you work with the letter J in Kabbalah, it produces a beautiful rainbow. When you work with the letter I, it produces a very, very, very beautiful rainbow. And the letter J in particular has a frequency of hugging, this is all I can say, as a metaphor. When people see it, they feel loved by it, it hugs them. And when you generate this frequency within yourself, you feel like you want to hug everybody.

I did this frequency for a one-year practice, I like to do one year per letter in Kabbalah. And I found myself becoming slightly gay, and it was kind of a weird experience that my body became soft, my personality became soft, my voice became slightly gay, not that this is a bad thing or a good thing, it's just what this frequency does to people. And some of my friends would say, you're not changing sides, are you? And I'd say, no, no, just a practice I'm doing at the moment, softening that masculine energy is becoming more softer and more feminine.

This frequency of love, it's seeking to balance electric and magnetic towards a type of equanimity where you equalise between the yang side and the inside, inside of the love. And that rainbow energy is the effect. So rainbow energy is an expression of compassion and love, which are similar frequencies.

Whatever practice you do where you're creating very, very high amounts of this magnetic fluid, you're going to generate a rainbow aura around you, especially if the information inside that magnetism is in resonance with universal love. And you're invoking prayer through the practice in resonance, universal love, a rainbow body will just start to appear around you and just become an actual part of your experience.

SOFB: Thank you very much for your time in providing such detailed responses.

wayne

Introduction to Wayne

Wayne is a life long practitioner having started practicing over four decades ago in the summer of 1977! This should point to the degree of experience that Wayne is bringing to this interview. His practice is well rounded in meditational practices, energy work and the martial arts being an experienced practitioner and teacher of Wing Chun.

Interview

SOFB: Welcome and thank you very much for agreeing to this interview. Please introduce yourself and let us know how you discovered the teachings of Franz Bardon.

Wayne: My real name is XXXX, in disguise as Wayne O'Boogie as I teach in the UK so my Students don't know who I am. Anyone who knows me well will understand my pseudonym. I live in the UK.

I was interested in Alchemy first (and still am). I read that Basil Valentine had said to study the Quabbalah to understand alchemy and the book of abramelin stated qabalah was the highest art. When I was a student in London (Studying Physics with Astrophysics at Queen Mary College, University of London) in the mid 1970s I went into an occult bookshop in South Kensington called "the Equinox" where I found a copy of *The Key to the True Quabbalah* by Franz Bardon. This kept referring to IIH and it wasn't long before I got that and the POME too. I started practicing IIH in the Summer of 1977 after I finished my first year exams.

I have studied, chi gung, dzogchen and I teach Wing Chun Kung Fu having studied with Sifu Shaun Rawcliffe and Master Ip Chun in Hong Kong. I recommend anyone who studies IIH also practice a martial art; they complement each other perfectly.

SOFB: If you had to design a curriculum to cover the contents of IIH and prepare a student for PME would you do anything differently to what is already in IIH.

Wayne: There are definite parts that you need to master, besides the preliminary exercises in chapters 1-2. For example invoking the elements, depth point meditations etc. Once these are mastered you can invoke the elements in all the places Bardon mentions, similarly for the depth point stuff. This would make IIH look far less daunting as there aren't that many fundamental practices that need to be mastered before they can be applied elsewhere. (Perhaps I'll write a guide on this in the future). I would then list each exercise in order in each step and indicate clearly which ones need to be practised daily until that becomes superseded, for example replacing vacancy of mind with the Akasha trance. A version of the mental wandering notes in POME could be included in IIH. A few uses for the personal depth point meditation (akasha trance) could be included in IIH from POME and TKTTTQ, although Rawn Clark gives some help on this in ABC (which I highly recommend as a guide to use as you proceed though IIH)

SOFB: The early steps 1-3 have a few sticking points like VOM, how clear a visualization should be and feeling the force of the vital force and elements. What tips can you give those currently struggling with these steps.

Wayne: Practice daily, regardless of how long as a few minutes will benefit you. Try to incorporate things into your daily life I was not a good visualizer and had to see/hear/feel the real things first then remember them afterwards; if it's cold outside I go and feel what it's like with full attention, then try to remember the feeling. Don't underestimate making up a ritual for this. I'm currently building the qabalah into mine but simple ones work too, for example, draw a tv screen with your forefinger and say "I see an apple" - do this every time you visualise and when the link is made it becomes easier.

SOFB: In my own journey I have found concentration to be key for many exercises. It was not that I could not do what was required it was just that I had not understood what is meant by quality and quantity. Could you talk about this subject and share how relevant or not it has been in your own journey to understand this concept.

Wayne: The key to concentration for me was awareness of the present moment. Try it now, put this article down and become totally aware of what's going on inside you (including your mind) and around you......

How did you do? Did you lose it and become distracted? How long did you manage? Ok, now you know what you're up against do it again and make more effort. I found doing this daily improved my concentration beyond belief. Development of concentration is a gradual process so don't beat yourself up about it.

List what you want out of IIH, look at it everyday and modify/change it as necessary but keep your eye on your goals, this will make you want them more, also make do-able short term goals to reach the big ones. This wanting is the quality. This is linked to actually doing the practices, you'll make more of an effort to actually do them if you know your goals, this is how I understand "quantity".

SOFB: At what point in the training (if any) did you realize that what was talked about by Franz Bardon is actually possible and not just a pleasant distraction?

Wayne: Once I worked on my Elemental Equilibrium things started working more consistently rather than haphazardly as it did previously. Development of clairvoyance gives you a huge realization - and I'm not particularly gifted in this - it takes work but it is improving for me, it shows the methods work and that the universe truely is a wondrous place.

SOFB: How has the work of IIH impacted your life?

Wayne: I feel it is a practice that can be incorporated into every aspect of daily life. My dzogchen teacher taught me to look at practices like that. I practice while standing in the queue at the checkout in Tesco, while pretending to watch TV, on long journeys etc., as well as my specified practice times. As a teacher I created a calm atmosphere in my classroom using vital life force (VLF), simple finger rituals to dissolve confrontational situations etc. I think of the practices in IIH as principles that can be used when the need arises as well as evolutionary tools.

A pupil once asked me (for an English project) "What book has had the most influence on me," My reply was IIH and that resulted in a number of pupils reading it. I never thought that would be the result!

SOFB: I see that you are also involved in alchemy. For those of us not familiar can you explain why you got involved in alchemy and how if at all it relates to the work of IIH, PME and KTQ.

Wayne: I had been reading about alchemy since I was 10. I have practiced it since my teens after getting the "Alchemist's Handbook" by Frater Albertus. As a result I have a laboratory in my garage and still practice today. I tend to view everything as alchemy, including IIH; it's an evolutionary process almost exactly adhering to solve-purify-coagula; just look at the steps, the early ones purify our body, soul and spirit individually (solve), the latter ones develop the presence of God within us and bring things all together; the human Philosophers' Stone. Don't overlook the laboratory work however, this illustrates, proves and illuminates the inner work.

SOFB: In addition to alchemy you are also a Martial Artist as many of us Bardonists appear to be. How has the IIH training impacted your Martial Arts? Has it inspired new methods approaches? Transformed what you had?

Wayne: Most definitely. Wing Chun (which I also teach) gives you a particular set of tools and once you understand them, it's up to you to make them work for you, in the process it also transforms you; it develops focus, humility, persistence etc. It's also a very economical system and I apply all these approaches to IIH. In return I find IIH develops qualities needed in Wing Chun such as internal energy, visualisation etc, a bit like a biofeed-back loop. It considerably helps with astral equilibrium.

SOFB Community Questions

SOFB Community: How do the concepts of electric and magnetic parts of the body, as described by Rawn Clark, relate to the potential existence of chakras? If the chakras do exist, can they be visually perceived by clairvoyant individuals in a similar way to how the electric and magnetic parts of the body can be perceived through personal development and experience?

Furthermore, what is your interpretation of Franz Bardon's statement in his book Initiation Into Hermetics that the muladhara chakra is an initiation diagram and corresponds to the first Tarot card? Does this imply that the chakras are simply a mental construct , serving as a map for the mind to traverse?

Wayne: I have not done much work on the Chakras and I think Rawn says somewhere that these develop and unblock naturally as you go through the steps in IIH so I don't really involve myself directly in them.

SOFB Community: Energy related questions.

What charging methods have you found to be most efficient in building up and retaining great amounts of energy.

In comparison to many methods of energy development in Taoist systems from China and Kejawen/Tenaga Dalem systems of Indonesia how important is the development, building up of and storage of energy in the Franz Bardon system as opposed to just using resources when it is needed.

For example, often the focus is upon filling lower dantien as precursor to microcosmic orbit or India/Tibet then working on successive chakras and the 3 channels.

Wayne: I have worked with the microcosmic orbit, Chi Gung and Tai Chi as well as some internal aspects of Wing Chun taught to me whilst in Hong Kong. In all of these practices I see similarities with IIH and tend to revert to them. Once you learn to accumulate VLF you can do many things with it including fill the dantien and circulate it (although there are far more interesting and useful things to do with it). Even chi gung masters get too full of chi (VLF) and use venting practices, I find it easier to get rid of it as Bardon suggests. Experiment, feel it and use that feeling as a guide if you feel tension and/or irritable etc, vent it.

SOFB Community: Do you believe in the existence of the Kundalini? If so have you awakened this power within yourself?

Wayne: I have had some feelings of awakening of Kundalini at times, I've just observed it with no attachment. Once again, I've not sought this; IIH practice is enough for me. My feeling is that kundalini rising is a natural occurrence and happens when certain conditions are met like removing blockages in your energy system. IIH does that as you progress through it.

SOFB Community: Are you able to talk about any experience with the beings of the second book?

Wayne: I have consulted some beings on alchemy practices, using methods of evocation like those used by Bill Mistele. I like to keep it simple and use a sort of dialogue; Vacancy of Mind is so important for this. I'm sorry but I can't talk any more on this due to an oath of silence on what information was obtained.

SOFB: Finally is there anything you feel we should have covered that we have missed? Please feel free to share here.

Wayne: Thank you for giving me the time and allowing me to speak on this. If anyone has any other specific questions please get in touch.

SOFB: Thank you for sharing Wayne.

MICHAEL LAMB

Introduction to Michael Lamb

Michael Lamb is an Kabbalistic Alchemist, having studied for nine years at The School of Inner Knowledge, with Hermetic Lore, Universal Healing, Colour, Sound, The Elements, Vibration, Numerology, Astronomy/ Astrology, Cosmology, Astral & Mental Projection, Occult Mysteries, Electro Magnetism, Ancient Eastern & Western Philosophy, Tarot, Kabbalah, Dozens of Meditation techniques & an Absolute Love for Life. He has appeared on several radio shows recorded meditations and taught in Europe, whilst visiting many Sacred sites.

Interview

SOFB: Welcome to Students of Franz Bardon. Thank you for taking the time for our questions. Let's start with your background. You mentioned that you began the work of *Initiation into Hermetics* before or during the 1980s. Can you please share your story about how you encountered Franz Bardon's teachings?

Michael Lamb: Yes, it was around '85 when I was training in martial arts and their associated philosophies. The discipline was intense, not like the Korean or Japanese systems. It was focused on one particular martial art and its approach. That's when I met my teacher, William Cook Edwards, who had a society called Tomorrow's World. He taught sensing to the students in the martial arts. Two schools had merged, and I joined them. One night, while reading a book called "One Pointedness of Concentration," I saw a person who looked exactly like the picture in the book. It turned out to be William. He recognized me and said I would become a great teacher someday, a prediction that has been validated by many students.

At the time, I didn't know who Franz Bardon was, but later I discovered that Bill had incorporated Bardon's work into the teachings of the School of Inner Knowledge. The school had just started with a small group of five or six students. On my first night, I was captivated by meditation, visualization, concentration, and understanding the depths of meditation itself, including the spirit, soul, astral body, mind, and physical body. We had classes once a week, then expanded to twice a week, including healing through Bardon's work. The School of Inner Knowledge covered about 70-80% of Bardon's book, along with additional nuances. I continued with the school until '95 when other responsibilities and personal growth compelled me to move on. Spending four to five years in a school is considered good progress before knowing it's time to explore and pursue individual paths.

The first night of my training was absolutely phenomenal, with simple yet profound teachings. Simple basics, a wonderful time. Young and enthusiastic, learning about emotions and their impact on the mind. We focused on balancing emotions and their connection to the elements - fire, earth, water, and ether. I started journaling, following Franz Bardon's suggestion of a psychic diary. In my journal, I explored the spirit and its energy, the astral body's connection to fire and the soul's connection to liquid energies. It all made sense to me, drawing from my knowledge of gods and goddesses and various realms. It was a period of accelerated learning and wisdom gained through experiences, relationships, and interactions with the elements. As the years went by, everything started to make sense at different levels. I delved into Zen, Taoism, Hinduism, Islam, Judaism, and Christianity, deepening my understanding of different philosophies and religions. Incorporating the elements into meditations was empowering, creating a transformative and euphoric experience. Learning about the pineal gland and medulla oblongata improved my seeing abilities, allowing me to perceive auras and energy fields. Teaching others to see and experience these phenomena brought me joy and was a blessing.

During certain moon phases, like the full moon, you can observe a green gold aura on the horizon as it rises. As it progresses higher, the colors shift to red, blue, violet, and purple. This is a good way to begin learning about auras. Seeing auras is just the starting point, though. In deeper meditation, your clairaudience develops as you listen attentively to your thoughts and feelings. Bill's classes incorporated a significant amount of *Initiation into Hermetics*, which I only discovered 20 years later when a friend, also a student, revealed that much of it was Franz Bardon's work. We worked with various beings, including nature spirits, earth spirits like gnomes and fire drakes, as well as air elemental spirits. Initially, it felt like fairy tales, but through the integration of other disciplines, it became a tangible reality. Working with these beings led to extraordinary experiences and accelerated progress. Connecting with the fifth element brought encounters with ETs and ancient races, from jinn to draconian races. It required immense power and energy to comprehend and navigate these energies. I have many stories to share about these experiences, but I'll cover them in subsequent questions. This was just the beginning, and after about six to seven months, we embarked on the work of KTQ, starting with the E and D exercises. I'm grateful, blessed, and humbled by this incredible journey of adventures and discoveries.

SOFB: What would you describe as the key skills or stages of development from *Initiation into Hermetics*?

Michael Lamb: The key skills or stages of development in *Initiation into Hermetics* can be described in a series of basics. Firstly, concentration and focus are essential, along with the ability to visualize and harness the power of imagination. Meditation is a fundamental practice in the initial stages, forming a triad with home, work, and play. Geometries, such as circles, triangles, squares, and more, come into play as well.

The next stage involves understanding the connection and adaptability of the five elements: fire, air, water, earth, and the fifth element (golden mean). These elements are infinite and timeless, granting access to the Time Matrix and toroidal fields. By going beyond the circle and entering a three-dimensional and eventually four-dimensional realm, profound insights about electromagnetism and the universe unfold.

Moving forward, the training intensifies, requiring dedicated focus and effort while also learning to flow with the rhythm of life. Each element plays a role: fire enables action, earth represents stability, water signifies adaptability, and air relates to emotional balance. The ether provides strategic approaches and harmonization with various systems or disciplines.

As the depth of training increases, one delves into vortexes of creation, encountering different life forces in realms and dimensions beyond. Psychic abilities are developed through rigorous practices, including reading for others and healing work. Trust in one-self and the Divine deepens, along with a sense of humor gained from the challenges faced. A comprehensive understanding of the elements and their layers is acquired, and color and sound become significant aspects, especially in the context of the true Kabbalah.

These are the key skills and stages at the beginning levels, and there is more to explore in subsequent layers. The journey involves a profound connection to the soul and the development of a keen perception of energy and its nuances. Thank you for the thought-provoking question.

SOFB: What shareable Insight has been the most significant regarding your training?

Michael Lamb: One of the greatest insights gained through the practice of harmonizing with various beings, including people, animals, elemental beings, and even advanced extraterrestrial or interdimensional entities, is the unveiling of the ancient true history of our planet and solar system. This knowledge often contradicts mainstream narratives. Additionally, developing the perception to see through mainstream media and societal conditioning becomes essential. The ability to maintain harmony even in challenging or dangerous situations is invaluable and has personally saved me many times.

Another profound insight is the experience of empathy and telepathic connection with family members who may not initially understand or believe in this work. Young children, animals, and even stones can sense the energy and authenticity we embody. Universal love and appreciation for all creations, as well as an understanding of the holographic nature of our universe, further expand our perception beyond the material plane.

It is difficult to pinpoint one specific significant insight as this journey encompasses numerous interconnected aspects. Daily gratitude, dream recollection, and the ability to provide understanding and guidance to others navigating their awakening process are gifts that come with this work. Sharing such experiences garners respect and fosters deep connections with those seeking assistance.

SOFB Community Questions

SOFB Community: How would you describe the best way to raise awareness and consciousness in daily life to avoid the automatic life?

Michael Lamb: To raise awareness and expand consciousness in daily life, it is crucial to recognize that everything happens for a reason and that we are interconnected with all things. Understanding the principle of cause and effect allows us to interact with people and circumstances consciously and choose our own path. By thinking beyond the limitations imposed by mainstream narratives, we tap into our natural rebellious spirit, questioning the status quo and seeking a deeper understanding of reality.

Embracing the concept of reincarnation and aiming for personal growth and resurrection, we transcend the state of merely surviving or being stuck in a state of limbo. Instead, we actively engage in creating our own reality and pursuing areas of expertise that align with our passions and stimulate our souls. Synchronicities and heightened awareness become prevalent, offering glimpses into other levels of consciousness. Exploring disciplines such as astrology, astronomy, and tarot can provide insight into the origins of these synchronicities.

Recalling and working with dreams is a valuable tool for awakening. Through dream work, we can achieve lucidity and awareness in the astral planes, preventing us from living an automatic life. While certain aspects of life may still operate on autopilot, engaging in conscious activities and being fully present in nature or engaging in meaningful conversations can enhance our conscious experience. By embracing these practices, we move away from a haphazard, average existence and cultivate a more awakened and intentional way of living.

Thank you for the excellent question.

SOFB Community: How can practitioners of Franz Bardon's step one exercises adapt and enhance their practice in light of the current world situation? Are there any specific comments or recommendations you would offer to complement Master Bardon's teachings in order to address the unique challenges and opportunities of today?

Michael Lamb: That's a great question. Things have changed significantly in many ways, but there are also similarities that persist. For instance, during the Second World War, Franz Bardon wrote *Frabato the Magician*, and it is well-known that Hitler sought to collaborate with him. Even when I began my own journey, initially unaware of Bardon's work, I was practicing a combination of *Initiation into Hermetics*, *The Practice of Magical Evocation*, and the *Key to the True Kabbalah*, along with tarot readings and pendulum work. The fundamentals remain relevant.

To advance these practices, it is important to focus on maintaining a good diet and exercise routine that suits you. Finding activities that stimulate you, such as spending time in nature and breathing in clean oxygen, can have a positive impact. Accessing high-quality foods, fruits, vegetables, and necessary supplements is not difficult. If you consume meat, ensure it is ethically sourced and approach it with a sense of gratitude and blessing. Posture and body cleansing rituals, like showering or immersing in natural bodies of water, can be elevated to meaningful acts of purification.

In preparation for interviews or conversations, I personally engage in simple mantras to align my energy, whether it be as a peacemaker, healer, communicator, or teacher. Polarity, encompassing the negative, positive, and neutral, is an important aspect to explore and understand. It is vital to find what works best for you through imitation, practice, and the guidance of reputable teachers, recognizing that there are both brilliant and mediocre ones. Mixing and matching various teachings and approaches is possible.

Researching the scientific backing behind these practices can be enlightening. The connection between dreams, meditation, and the alleviation of negative emotions is supported by scientific evidence. Additionally, advanced extraterrestrial races and anti-gravity technology have been present for decades, although much has been concealed. Exploring the realms of high-end mysteries, colors, and sounds can expand our understanding. Just as learning scales on a musical instrument paves the way for creative expression, mastering the basics of these practices lays a solid foundation.

Harmony has always been my preferred approach. Harmonizing with situations and adapting oneself accordingly is a powerful skill. Despite the increased censorship in the current digital era, the internet remains a valuable resource for knowledge. While the search for ancient wisdom may resemble combing through old libraries for hidden spells, modern teachings have become more streamlined and relevant. Trust your intuition when seeking out speakers, books, and resources.

If you would like further guidance, feel free to reach out to me. I can assist you in streamlining your studies and embracing different energies. Thank you for the excellent question.

SOFB Community: What was your most important breakthrough?

Michael Lamb: You may wonder why we start with Step 1. When we worked with *Initiation into Hermetics*, it wasn't simply about going through the book page by page or chapter by chapter. It was a continuous process that spanned months and even years, always returning to the foundational teachings. It's not a linear progression where you learn the early chapters and then move on; it's more like a cycle of advancing and revisiting those fundamentals. Even as you delve into more advanced practices like color and sound combinations or the qualitative and quantitative aspects of the 72 or 144 Names of God, the *Initiation into Hermetics* remains essential.

One significant breakthrough for me was realizing that the fantasy world is real, while what the mainstream media presents is often false. It was a transformative moment when I recognized the truth about extraterrestrial races visiting our planet—a massive secret that can no longer be hidden. I understand that this may be too far-fetched for some, but for those who delve deeper and embrace this knowledge, it can be mind-blowing. The truth is hidden in plain sight, known by those who hold power, but there are numerous powerful forces at play. It's like a cosmic battle for control of this planet—an eye-opening revelation.

Over time, I came to understand that there are only a few families behind the financial institutions, and that's why things are so messed up. Many controlling elements operate behind the scenes in different countries. However, amidst these challenges, there are also opportunities to practice our work. This breakthrough helped me realize that everything ultimately stems from love—the driving force of the universe. Yet, there are entities seeking to hijack power, energy, and the soul force by feeding on negativity. It's astonishing to see the coexistence of incredible, benevolent beings with immense energy and knowledge alongside malicious entities that thrive on fear and the life force of others. This understanding can be gained through meditation and reveals the immense power of our planet and the extraordinary times we live in.

The breakthrough lies in becoming aware of the love that permeates everything while simultaneously confronting the harsh realities of how the material world is governed and the factors at play. It unveils a cosmic hierarchy or power struggle. It's truly an awakening experience, complementing your own skills and enabling you to make a difference in this world. With this work, you can move mountains, but there may be some mountains you cannot shift. I hope this provides a greater awareness that aligns with your question. It's an excellent inquiry, and I appreciate the opportunity to address it. Thank you.

SOFB Community: What would you advise a young student in regards to the uncontrolled water emotions?

Michael Lamb: That's a great question, and it encompasses various aspects related to love, both in a material sense and in our connections with beings and things we hold dear. Love extends to plants, crystals, old friends, and the animal kingdom. It also includes powerful emotions we experience in our relationships with others. Love can be explored from different angles, but one of the most significant aspects is universal love, which goes beyond the material and encompasses the realm of sexuality and desires.

Our love for sex and desires is part of our nature and often influences our lustful tendencies. However, it can also be channeled into a disciplined practice, especially when we appreciate the beauty of living in a physical body. In the past, there was even a book in the Bible called the Book of Jubilees, celebrating humankind and our expression of sexual and sensual pleasures. These experiences are closely connected to the water element and emotions, particularly for individuals with certain zodiac signs like Scorpio, Pisces, and Cancer.

Water, with its magnetic qualities, is not easily describable, but it holds great power. Our bodies are composed of various liquids, such as tears, perspiration, blood, sexual fluids, plasma, and more. Each of these liquids has its own consistency, viscosity, and temperament. Understanding the density and viscosity of these liquids helps us grasp their significance. Our magnetic nature comes into play as we are instantly drawn to certain beings and repelled by others, creating a balance of attraction and repulsion.

When powerful emotions like love arise, particularly in the astral plane, there is a tremendous amount of energetic activity resembling fireworks or spiraling colors of magnetism. It's a psychedelic experience, where sparks and magnetism fill the space. Observing, feeling, and acknowledging this energy is important in recognizing its presence and impact.

It's worth exploring the constellations, planets, and specific emotions to gain a deeper understanding of this phenomenon.

Working with magnetism is an incredible energy to harness, and it strengthens our individuality and personal magnetism. Acknowledging our weaknesses and admiring them as part of our nature allows us to strive for balance. Engaging with water rituals, such as immersing oneself in cold mountain streams or early morning ocean swims, can be powerful practices to cleanse and balance our energy. Using magnetism to balance magnetism or fire to fight fire is often effective.

I hope this answers your question, although there is much more to discuss and explore on a deeper level. By understanding and detecting these emotions more quickly, you can embark on your own adventures, becoming a stronger individual with your balanced magnetism. Working with magnetic energy is transformative, and appreciating the role of liquids in this process can be profound. Thank you for this lovely question. Cheers!

SOFB Community: I would like the interviewee to elaborate on the following topics:

1. **The Kundalini process and its significance.**

2. **Development of the Third Eye and any physical substances that can aid in its activation.**

3. **The use of Qigong or similar physical practices to enhance and circulate energy.**

4. **The interviewee's experience and insights on working with talismans.**

5. **Advice on self-defense at the astral level, specifically drawing from Bardon's work.**

Thank you.

Michael Lamb: Alright, let's tackle your questions one by one. First, let's delve into the fascinating connection between the Kundalini process and the development of the third eye. When the Kundalini energy awakens, it works with the seven main chakras, represented by the colors of the rainbow: red for the base chakra, orange for the sacral chakra, yellow for the solar plexus chakra, green for the heart chakra, blue for the throat chakra, indigo for the third eye chakra, and violet for the crown chakra. As the energy rises, it creates a beautiful rainbow effect, activating and balancing each chakra.

Opening the third eye, in particular, holds great significance. In my personal experience, during the training I underwent, we associated the third eye with the planet Uranus. When my third eye opened, I vividly remember perceiving a distinct pinkish-violet color. It was a powerful and transformative moment for me, although I must emphasize that this process can vary for individuals and requires adequate preparation and understanding.

Moving on to physical condensers, incorporating essential vitamins like magnesium and vitamin K can greatly benefit your overall well-being. It's also beneficial to expose yourself to sunlight and connect with nature early in the day to ground your physicality. Consuming vital greens and probiotics is recommended, and you can even create your own physical condensers using high-quality foods in your kitchen. Anointing your body with coconut oil, which is affordable and nourishing for the skin, while performing ritualistic prayers and movements, can further enhance your practice.

To amplify and circulate energy, engaging in physical practices such as Qigong, Tai Chi, or other stretching exercises is valuable. By tuning into your body and its anatomy, as discussed in Bardon's work, you can better understand the impact of nutrition and energy flow on various bodily systems. Talismans, including crystals and metals, can play a role in enhancing your practice. For instance, a silver ring with an amethyst can serve as a simple yet powerful talisman. Additionally, wearing breathable clothing in colors that resonate with your energy and mood can contribute to your overall well-being.

When it comes to self-defense at the astral level, maintaining a foundation of high-quality nutrition, clean thoughts, and clean living is crucial. By nourishing your body with oils and colors that suit you, you create an armor of positive energy. Regular meditation, focused on the higher good of the planet, can help you avoid unnecessary conflicts. It's also important to be mentally prepared with comebacks in various situations, ranging from calm and balancing responses to assertive retorts. Striking the right balance is key, and it's a skill that requires practice and self-awareness.

Psychic self-defense and protection are vast topics that warrant individual exploration. It's essential to road test various techniques to find what resonates with you personally. While I've provided a brief overview here, I encourage you to dive deeper into these subjects and seek personalized guidance to develop a robust self-defense and protection practice that aligns with your unique journey.

SOFB Community: What experience does Michael have with the physical manifestation of the elements? And if successful at this? Did he have to make any changes in the training detailed in *Initiation into Hermetics* by Franz Bardon?

Michael Lamb: That's an excellent question because the physical manifestation of the elements is one of the most practiced areas in my life. It has brought me tremendous success and health, although I've also faced challenges along the way, especially when I started recording CDs. In fact, I'm currently in the studio tonight with my friend and colleague, Cameron Street, who greatly assists me in tuning up the elements. We've recorded several CDs focusing on the elements, planets, and their connection to constellations. However, working with the elements in the microcosm has been particularly fantastic for manifesting success.

A crucial aspect of manifestation is maintaining a happy and healthy connection with your family and friends. Equally important is finding solace in solitude and nurturing your own individuality. The elements are present in every nanosecond, forming the very fabric of time itself. They encompass gravity and other fundamental forces, constantly entering and exiting our lives and realms in their individual form. Therefore, I would emphasize the significance of establishing a profound connection with elemental beings in nature, particularly in the oceans, streams, and serene country recesses.

My personal journey has also involved extensive connections with advanced extraterrestrial races, diverse guides, genii, and principles. The omens have played a pivotal role in navigating these realms and establishing connections with various living beings. Furthermore, they have enabled me to delve deeper into my own color and sound spells, contributing to personal growth and enhancing my daily life experiences.

Whether one seeks to manifest material desires or other aspirations, there are specific spells associated with each element. These spells are intertwined with the corresponding colors and sounds, perpetuating a continuous cycle. For comprehensive insights and practical guidance, I highly recommend exploring Franz Bardon's work, which provides detailed instructions. I have personally tested and continue to engage with these practices on a daily basis, as the elements form an inseparable part of my existence.

I have conducted numerous workshops, shedding light on the manifestations of the elements and their profound influence on the physical, mental, emotional, and Akashic aspects of our being. Additionally, I am constantly refining my CDs, revisiting and recording the elements to ensure their accurate representation. Working with the elements has become an integral part of my daily routine, as they are the very foundation of our existence. Without them, life as we know it would not be possible.

I appreciate your thought-provoking question, and I hope this response provides you with a clearer understanding of the tremendous impact and ongoing exploration of the elements in my life's journey.

SOFB Community: Michael, what is your daily hermetic training regime.

Michael Lamb: I still follow the harmony ritual, which is quite simple. It involves harmonizing with the day and the upcoming situations, as well as the people I will be meeting. I make an effort to stretch as much as possible, especially on days when I have a tight schedule. This includes push-ups, sit-ups, and various stretching exercises, followed by a calming meditation.

In my practice, I incorporate the five elements and the five Platonic solids, along with the constellations and central chakras. This combination creates a layered meditation approach, comprising around 20 or 30 meditations. It suits me well due to its ease and practicality.

For instance, when working with the fire element, I visualize not only the triangle in the head region, as described by Barden, but also the tetrahedron. This connects me with Aries, Leo, and Sagittarius. Moving on to the air element, I visualize the octahedron in the chest area, rather than just the inverted triangle with a line through it. This aligns with Gemini, Libra, and Aquarius. Then, I transition to the icosahedron, representing the water element, instead of just the inverted triangle or the feminine aspect. This relates to Scorpio, Pisces, and Cancer (or what I like to call Teesha). Lastly, I focus on the cube, representing the earth element in the body, starting from the top of the thighs and extending to the toes. In this practice, I expand the visualization of the cube, acknowledging its three-dimensional nature and its significance in ceremonial magic. This corresponds to Taurus, Virgo, and Capricorn.

To incorporate all elements, I visualize the dodecahedron as the fifth element. Rather than just seeing it as a five-point star or a six-point star, I perceive it as two tetrahedrons merging to form a three-dimensional pentagram. This understanding helps me grasp the intricate workings of crystals within this planet and beyond, including the various dimensions. It also allows for instant access to colors and other associated elements, creating a comprehensive and efficient practice that resonates with me.

In addition to these practices, I create small mandalas for specific occasions or surprises that may arise. Sometimes, my routine may vary or be disrupted due to laziness or busyness, but I quickly regret it and make a conscious effort to return to my practice. I remind myself not to succumb to the complexities of guilt and instead prioritize consistent and dedicated work.

Overall, this is my daily regime, and I find great joy and satisfaction in leading this lifestyle. It has brought me tremendous happiness and contentment thus far.

SOFB Community: What advice would you give yourself if you could go back to the 1980s, during your time as a beginner doing *Initiation into Hermetics*?

Michael Lamb: My advice would be to avoid laziness and not give up. Trust that you are embarking on a remarkable journey that can bring wealth, health, and success in various areas. However, it is important to consider the cost of these achievements. I would have liked to be more aware, but looking back at how far I've come and the mistakes I've made, I have learned to embrace them. Living a life without regrets is crucial as regret can be detrimental to the soul. So, instead of dwelling on what I would change, I am content with certain aspects I wouldn't alter. The advice I would give my past self is to love oneself more and dedicate more effort to working with colors and sounds, as they can provide significant assistance. Additionally, it is essential to trust your intuition. I have had many instances where intuition guided me in making wise investment decisions, offering help, or persevering in relationships. That would be the advice I'd share with my younger self.

SOFB Community: Michael, in your opinion, is there anything that could greatly accelerate the progress in practice?

Michael Lamb: I mentioned this earlier, but I'll provide a more detailed response. When engaging in physical exercise, pay attention to your breathing. Focus on exhaling deeply, allowing oxygen to reach your bloodstream and promoting a connection with nitrogen. This not only frees the mind but also enhances the flow of clean breath throughout your body. While performing exercises like sit-ups, push-ups, swimming, cycling, or stretching, visualize energy flowing through your body.

This visualization amplifies the effects of your workout and can be applied to specific areas you wish to develop. For instance, if you want to enhance your connection with a particular element, build up that element's energy within you and release it during your practice. These foundational techniques are crucial, and it is important to master them before exploring more advanced methods.

Returning to the basics, known as the five fundamentals, is essential. Additionally, pay attention to your nutrition as it plays a significant role in maintaining happiness. Without proper nutrition, genuine joy may become challenging to sustain. Surround yourself with joyous and inspiring individuals whenever possible, as their presence can positively impact your energy. Titanium and sapphires are effective for amplifying energy, and it's important to work with them while maintaining clarity. Be cautious, as amplifying negative emotions can lead to unwanted consequences. Bless your living space, charge your working areas with your energy, and release negative thought forms and energies when you're finished with them. Minimize interactions with energy-draining individuals, although it may not always be avoidable.

Embrace your own company and cultivate self-love and gratitude. Gratitude has the power to open up and exponentially increase energy levels. While I could discuss additional exercises at length, these recommendations should serve as a starting point for beginners.

If you'd like to delve deeper into this topic, feel free to reach out to James, and we can have another conversation.

SOFB Community: Michael, when it comes to the physical manifestation of the Akasha, are there any side effects associated with heavy or excessive use? I'm not referring to its abuse or misuse, but rather the potential effects on the student or members, particularly in relation to the Saturn zone and other locations.

Michael Lamb: Alright, let's delve into this question. It's a bit peculiar, but I'll break it down for you.

We're discussing the physical manifestation of Akasha and whether it has any side effects. The Akashic plane is where we access the records to learn about timelines, the true history of the planet, and even glimpse into the future. Akasha can be seen as a distinct dimension of ether, separating the elements and having its own unique consistency.

Personally, I've always treated it with respect and haven't experienced many negative effects from overuse. It's crucial to approach Akasha with reverence and awareness of its ability to accelerate karma. Fortunately, I've had ample opportunities in this life to balance and disperse my karmic load over many years. Of course, karma can resurface, particularly in relationships and the Saturn zone. I've learned to anticipate these challenges, often occurring around specific times like the Ides of March.

Dealing with karmic energy requires acknowledging its Saturnian nature and the influence it has on our emotional well-being. Excessive use of Akasha can intensify potential karmic risks since it taps into a finite energy source. If one becomes too entangled in the material plane, difficulties may arise. To release and balance the energy, it is helpful to connect with Jupiter or Uranus, visualizing a cone or triangle within the body to harmonize all energy channels. Finding equilibrium and moderation in accessing Akasha, as with any element, color, or sound, is crucial. You must be your own governor, making conscious choices based on your understanding of the consequences involved.

SOFB Community: Michael, the optimal order of ways of practicing the letters (KTQ) to get the best mastery and insights of their nature.

Michael Lamb: Alright, let's delve into this question. It's quite extensive due to the complexity of the true Kabbalah. In terms of mastery of the letters, I found the letter D (dark blue) to be particularly powerful. It connects to the physical, mental, and astral planes. When I first experienced its energy, it was a profound and transformative moment. I also have an affinity for the letters E and A, and occasionally I go through all the letters, colors, and sounds, as there are 26 letters, 618 colors, and 60 sounds to explore.

Additionally, I consider the unrevealed 28th letter, which represents the four sevens. While I primarily follow Bardon's work, I've expanded my knowledge of colors and sounds through the School of Inner Knowledge. There are certain letters that resonate with me, such as the blood red M, the ultramarine K, and the silver blue H. Light violet is another favorite of mine. However, there are some letters I don't connect with as strongly, and I prefer not to discuss them as I don't use them extensively.

Regarding damaging or traumatic experiences, it depends on how one approaches the energy and whether they properly release it. Life itself presents challenges and traumas, regardless of one's practice with energy. The key lies in effectively managing stress and trauma rather than avoiding them altogether. There are remarkable healing aspects associated with certain letters, such as the light blue A, which I perceive as the sky, representing clarity and infinite potential. I've witnessed its healing effects in various situations, including decompression on aircraft and working with children.

Each individual can explore the letters in their own way, whether following the book or incorporating personal interpretations and combinations. I have discovered and utilized double and triple combinations that work well for me. Some additional combinations were taught in the School of Inner Knowledge in the 80s and 90s but were later phased out due to the complexity for newer students. As the school grew, we focused more on planes and dimensions. While I've shared the letters I favor, delving into the depth of each letter would require extensive time and workshops. Each letter has its own layers and planes of significance. I hope this provides some insight.

SOFB Community: Michael, have you personally experienced any side effects or direct impacts on yourself from dealing with elementals and elementaries?

Michael Lamb: Okay, this is a complex question, but I'll do my best to address it. Elementals and elementaries, or what Bardon refers to as manufacturing elementaries and what I personally call elementals, have had various effects on me. I have created a few of these beings, but eventually shifted my focus more towards working with nature spirits, which has been a rewarding experience.

Dealing with elemental spirits in powerful locations like Mount Warning or the beaches in Northern Rivers, New South Wales, has resulted in numerous magical encounters. I have captured many of these beings in photographs, and I am currently working on a book and DVD to showcase these connections and effects. When you begin to perceive the faces in stones and the life in water, everything becomes alive. Respecting and appreciating the power and energy of these larger and smaller beings earns you credibility in their realm.

At times, thoughts of ending or withdrawing from certain aspects of life may arise, influenced by the energies picked up from others. However, such actions are not permitted within the realms. Unusual patterns and issues have emerged in my life, including lightning strikes and encounters with extraterrestrial activity and elemental beings. These experiences may seem fantastical to those who haven't encountered them, but they hold significant meaning and impact for those involved. I've also had extraordinary experiences while in the ocean, such as paddling out to greet whales, being surrounded by telepathic dolphins, and witnessing lightning strikes during workshops.

These are just a few examples, and sharing all of my experiences would require a dedicated workshop. Each encounter has contributed to my growth and expanded my understanding of higher energies and knowledge.

SOFB Community: (Multiple questions from same person) Question: How do you imbue a condensed quality with an abstract and vague idea or intention, such as waterfalls or elemental fluids?

Michael Lamb: To imbue a condensed quality with an abstract and vague idea or intention, I prefer using raw elements like ether or electromagnetic energy instead of specific elements. While it's important to have a clear intention, if it's not well-defined, you can broaden the boundaries or scope to increase the chances of achieving your desired outcome. However, the specific process and timeframe for achieving the effects would depend on individual circumstances, making it difficult to provide a precise answer without more information.

Part B: How can a condensed quantity renew itself until complete recovery is reached?

Michael Lamb: When it comes to regenerative energy, I find it more effective to work with ether, platonic solids, and elemental constellation qualities. These energies have constant access to renewal and regeneration. However, the process of energy regeneration is complex, influenced by factors like time, space, and gravity. It's crucial to monitor and understand the consequences associated with working with these energies.

Part C: How can abstract ideas, visualizations, and rational states become more familiar and clearly defined?

Michael Lamb: To make abstract ideas, visualizations, and rational states more familiar and clearly defined, it's necessary to explore those realms and gain personal experiences. Working with the highest life forces on the planet can help in tuning into these qualities. Additionally, practicing lucid dreaming and astral projection can provide valuable insights and make these abstract concepts more tangible. Trusting the universe and expanding one's perception beyond the three-dimensional realm are essential in fully comprehending and integrating these qualities. Mastering time and gravity at the quantum level can also aid in understanding and working with abstract ideas and qualities.

SOFB Community: Praying, how should we incorporate this into our practice?

Michael Lamb: Okay, let's break down and explain the question about praying and its correct practice in hermetic practices. Praying, in the normal use by magically untrained individuals, doesn't imply weakness, but rather a lack of awareness and sovereignty over their own power and energy. When people pray, they often ask for something they lack or desire, sometimes without offering anything in return. This act is usually done with humility and gratitude, whether directed towards a divine being or a higher power. However, it's important not to generalize or judge individuals as weak because everyone's circumstances and understanding vary.

In hermetic practices, prayers are still a form of asking, whether it's to a specific being or a higher divine entity. The more specific the focus, the more specific the response may be. It's essential to recognize that there are numerous gods, goddesses, and divine entities, each with their own unique qualities and attributes. Understanding the true nature of these beings and working with specific energies, such as planetary beings, can lead to more effective results.

Having a belief system and faith is crucial in any practice, as it provides a framework for manifestation. The correct practice of prayer in hermetic practices involves cultivating pure love, gratitude, kindness, and devotion. It's a process that connects with the life force and utilizes energy channels through geometric shapes and potent symbols. By accessing and channeling energy more efficiently, prayers can manifest faster and with greater effectiveness.

The practice of prayer can evolve into a meditative function, where contemplation and clean energy channels are used to connect with higher realms and access vast amounts of energy. It's important to choose words carefully, as they can carry different meanings and energies. Prayer should be approached with the purest intent and highest thoughts, aligning with the greatest good and positive outcomes.

SOFB Community: What are the most effective physical practices, such as postures, movements, and exercises, recommended by Michael for fully dissolving tensions, opening up the body through tendons, ligaments, and muscles, and accumulating and condensing various energies within the body?

Michael Lamb: To effectively dissolve physical issues in the body, visualizations play a crucial role. Practices such as Qigong, Tai Chi, basic martial arts postures, and stretching exercises are highly beneficial. Simple stretching exercises can include neck stretches, rolling the neck, and leaning the arms over. As you perform these exercises, visualize the energy flowing through your body, channeling it through your chakras, hand chakras, and foot chakras. Visualize the energy moving from heaven to earth and back, permeating your entire physical body and opening up the tendons and ligaments.

Yoga and other disciplines that focus on opening the tendons and ligaments can also be helpful. Nutrition plays a vital role, so choose foods that support your body's needs based on your blood type. Additionally, your thoughts and intentions are essential in accumulating and condensing various energies throughout your body. You can incorporate colors and sounds associated with the Kabbalah, such as visualizing dark violet flowing through your spine and encompassing your entire body.

Remember that the body consists of multiple layers, including the lymphatic, muscular-skeletal, and respiratory systems, among others. Each layer can be influenced by different elemental combinations and corresponding colors and sounds. Dark blue, green, and light violet are recommended colors to work with, but explore the elemental color and sound combinations described in the *Key to the True Kabbalah* to find what resonates with you.

You can create a rainbow effect by incorporating various colors, or even experiment with the entire alphabet of colors for a comprehensive approach. Tuning into your body and understanding its unique needs can help maintain an ageless quality. Consider adding vitamins, minerals, and supplements that align with your body's requirements. Additionally, essential oils can be beneficial. Delve into the *key to the true Kabbalah* for more insights on effective color combinations.

In summary, there are numerous physical practices and techniques to explore, including Eastern practices like yoga, which can complement your understanding of occult anatomy. It would require a comprehensive workshop to fully delve into these practices and their basics.

SOFB Community: How to approach teaching or gradually initiating one's relatives, siblings and parents without revealing to them your practices and your actual spiritual beliefs.

Michael Lamb: This question raises an important and challenging aspect of guiding others away from dysfunctionality and towards a more peaceful path. It particularly focuses on the difficulties involved when it comes to one's family and close friends. Implementing this type of work is not a straightforward matter. Gradually introducing and initiating your relatives, siblings, and parents without explicitly revealing your spiritual practices and experiences can be a complex task.

One approach that comes to mind is subtly influencing their surroundings, such as energetically charging their rooms at night to facilitate the exteriorization of the mental or astral body during sleep. This could potentially help them believe in the existence of an afterlife. It is important to start slowly and cautiously due to the potential labeling and judgment that may arise when discussing such matters openly. The idea is to take baby steps or use a drip-feed approach, as you aptly mentioned. It takes time, sometimes even decades, to navigate these dynamics.

Finding ways to provide initiations or spiritual experiences for them while they are asleep can make it easier to reveal your own spiritual journey to them eventually. The questions posed demonstrate a loving and thoughtful approach, which resonates deeply and personally. Utilizing subtle awakening techniques involving colors and sounds, such as the softness of the letter "W," can be effective triggers. Combining it with the double "O" sound, like the gentle "whoo," can create a powerful combination. However, it's crucial to remember that if you introduce these techniques, you should also be prepared to remove them if necessary. If individuals experience spiritual awakening too abruptly without the proper grounding, it can lead to confusion and difficulty connecting the dots.

Families and siblings can be the most challenging to guide because of the strong desire for their well-being. If they are not yet awakened or lack a solid foundation like yours, introducing spiritual experiences too quickly can overwhelm them. They may encounter phenomena they don't understand, such as seeing ghosts or encountering past loved ones, without knowing how to make sense of it all. The key is to keep it subtle and allow them to connect the dots in their own time, like a slow-release granule of awakening. It's crucial to provide them with the right mental, emotional, and nutritional support to help them integrate these experiences into their reality at the appropriate time.

To fully explore this topic and discuss specific practices and subtle approaches, a one-on-one conversation would be beneficial. I would be happy to engage in a more detailed discussion with you or other members who have deeper connections to provide further guidance on this matter. Please reach out to James.

SOFB Community: Michael, based on your perspective thus far, what knowledge, resources, skills, siddhis, etc., do you consider necessary and beneficial for members to possess in light of emerging technologies such as robotic AI (artificial intelligence), VR (virtual reality), high tech, big data, transhumanism, and the integration of bio-digital life?

Michael Lamb: Okay, let's simplify the question. Michael, from your perspective, what knowledge, resources, and skills do you believe would be necessary and beneficial for individuals to navigate the future trends of robotic AI, big tech, bio-digital transhumanism, and other emerging technologies? For example, the person asking the question suggests advanced psychic empathy, telepathy, invisibility, and levitation as potential skills to cultivate. While these abilities may be challenging to develop physically, they should be considered.

However, the main focus of the question revolves around the skills and resources required to address the increasing influence of AI and virtual reality. These technologies are already shaping our lives, with social media and data collection being used to feed into powerful supercomputers. The entertainment industry has also subtly introduced concepts like half-human, half-robot beings, preparing us for the future. While technology aids us, we must remain aware of those controlling it, as the aim is for machines to dominate and transhumanism is already becoming a reality.

Alongside empathy and telepathy, working with sound and color combinations for protection can be valuable. Additionally, crystals and metals can be used for their unique properties, similar to the themes found in adventure movies. Ultimately, our approach to AI should involve recognizing that machines are like another phase or element, akin to the five elements in the East or the four elements and ether in the West. Metals, which are present in our bodies, represent intelligence and are also found in robots. Our attachment to technology, be it a car, computer, or other devices, stems from perceiving them as having a life force and creative energy. Nanobot technology and the spiritual aspects of technology are interconnected, and it is up to individuals to choose what aspects they are ready to embrace. This question encompasses various topics that would require a comprehensive workshop or discussion to explore fully.

SOFB Community: Michael, how can individuals who have a strong connection to water elementals in nature, possessing heightened empathy, a watery root chakra, and captivating auric and astral fields, protect themselves from unwanted attention and stalking by ordinary people who are drawn to their energizing presence?

Michael Lamb: That's a great question, and I'll address it. Let me break it down for better clarity. How can individuals who have both physical genders and are born with rare watery root and sacral chakras, along with a nearly superhuman level of empathy, protect themselves in everyday life from people of all genders who are unknowingly drawn to them and end up stalking them due to their irresistible magnetism and allure?

These individuals possess a strong magnetism associated with their connection to the liquid energies and astral fields. It's almost impossible for others to resist this attraction, both physically and on various levels. To protect themselves, they need to learn how to repel or neutralize this energy. One approach is to freeze or use the opposite polarity of the magnet, like a high spell. Elemental defense mechanisms, such as combining the letters E and N, as found in the Keys to the True Kabbalah, can also be effective. Additionally, tapping into etheric energy and drawing upon the blue-green energies of their watery chakras can provide further protection. It's crucial for them to understand and manage their powerful magnetism.

In terms of their high sex drives and impulses, beyond the usual means of burning off energy through sex and similar activities, they can explore alternative approaches. They can harness the energy of orgasm, where the soul and spirit unite for brief moments, and use it for their greater protection and to attract the right kind of people to work with. This isn't about being holier-than-thou, but rather about utilizing and transforming their energies for practical purposes. By raising and understanding these energies, they can transmute and direct them for healing, shielding, or attracting positive experiences.

Considering their unique energetic configuration, it might be helpful to explore astrology, such as their Venus placement in Gemini or Scorpio, to gain further insights. Understanding and working with the changing qualities of color and sound energies associated with water can also assist in balancing and utilizing their abilities.

SOFB Community: How can we best learn physical skills or martial arts when the tasks require a significant demand on our bodies and capacities? Some claim that mediumship is the most effective approach, but also the most physically draining. If this is true, how can we address and mitigate such challenges?

Michael Lamb: What is the best way to learn physical skills or martial arts? When the intensity of the training takes a toll on our bodies, it's time to explore our options. Personally, I would lean towards methods that soften the martial arts experience. You don't have to stick to hardcore practicality, like intense Aikido or Jujitsu. Instead, consider a gentler approach, such as a softer version of Aikido, Tai Chi, or even yoga. This way, you can still pursue your passion for martial arts while reducing the physical strain.

Now, if you're truly dedicated to the hardcore martial arts path, you'll need to prioritize the protection of your body. This is where your knowledge of shielding spells and capacities from the work of *Initiation into Hermetics* comes in handy. Ask for your body to be shielded and safeguarded during your training sessions.

There's another perspective to consider: some claim that mediumship is the ultimate way to learn physical skills. Mediumship can indeed come naturally to certain individuals, exuding vibrancy. However, it can also be physically draining for others. The crucial point here is energy replenishment. If mediumship is particularly draining for you, it implies that you might need to reevaluate how you replenish your energy from the universe. It's true that you absorb the energies of others, and sometimes those energies can be heavy. Learning to shed them quickly and efficiently is essential. I understand that it can be a bit challenging at first, but remember, as a medium, your role is to become a neutral pillar, balancing the positive and negative energies of others and finding that middle ground.

Similarly, with your martial arts practice, aim to find that middle ground that works best for you and aligns with your desires. If you genuinely wish to pursue both martial arts and mediumship, you need to strike a balance. Allow one to offset the physical demands of the other. Even though you might still experience stress and tension, effective management is key.

Choose potent spells that swiftly replenish your energy. I would recommend considering the fifth element (E) and harnessing the power of dark violet. But be mindful of your emotions as you build and release this energy. Find a rhythm of replenishment and release that works for you to effectively manage and offset the physical demands of both practices.

Remember, the answers to your questions lie within your own words. If mediumship can offset the physicality of martial arts, then find that middle ground where they can coexist without draining you. It's a clever revelation on your part! So, choose your path wisely, and utilize the most potent spells that replenish your energy rapidly. Keep in mind the importance of balancing and releasing your emotions as you build that energy.

SOFB Community: Are there any practices in Hermetics similar to Tummo, Trul Khor, and heat Yoga? If so, what benefits do these practices offer to practitioners?

Michael Lamb: Okay, once again, this is an excellent question. Practices like Tummo, Trul Khor, and heat Yoga are fantastic for releasing energy and toning the body. While I don't have extensive expertise in these specific practices, I have friends who engage in them. Personally, I focus on Tai Chi and various stretching exercises that work well for my body. Each practice carries its own unique benefits, and it's essential to discover what suits your anatomy and preferences.

Regarding Hermetics, there might not be direct equivalents, but there are overlapping principles and techniques that can be integrated. Franz Bardon, a prominent Hermetic practitioner, acknowledged the significance of Hindu and Buddhist practices like Yantras, mantras, and mudras. By combining different practices and techniques, you can create a comprehensive approach that aligns with Hermetic principles.

The duration of practice depends on your personal limits and preferences. Some individuals engage in intense bodybuilding for extended periods, while others prefer shorter, regular sessions. It's crucial to listen to your body and find a balance that works for you.

Engaging in these physical disciplines can have profound effects on the physical, astral, mental, and emotional bodies. By developing a deep connection with your physical body and expanding your awareness to your fingertips and toes, you can enhance your ability to access the astral body in dream states. This can lead to lucid dreaming, easier manipulation of the astral body, and skills like remote viewing. The benefits extend beyond the physical realm, offering a wide range of possibilities.

I hope this answer provides the clarity you were seeking. If you have any further questions, feel free to ask.

SOFB Community: How to cultivate unshakable conviction and faith in our minds correctly?

Michael Lamb: I would strongly recommend that you seek these insights through personal experience. Engaging in various practices and exercises can be beneficial, but nothing compares to firsthand encounters with the unseen and life-altering experiences. It is in these moments that you gain a profound understanding of what lies beyond conventional perception. Witnessing what is considered unseeable and grasping the true nature of the world provides a solid foundation of conviction.

However, this is not something that can be handed to you or obtained through external means. The unshakable faith and unwavering conviction stem from a deep trust in oneself and the universe, as well as a clear sense of purpose and direction. It is through this trust and conviction that you can cultivate a strong connection to your ancestral lineage and the future generations. This multi-faceted approach encompasses various elements and cannot be reduced to a single miraculous solution.

Ultimately, your best bet lies in your own direct experiences of perceiving the unseen, feeling the unfathomable, and hearing the unheard. Those who possess heightened clairvoyance, clairaudience, and clairsentience abilities have the potential to develop unwavering faith and conviction based on their own encounters and realizations.

Embrace the path of personal exploration and discovery, as it is through your own experiences that you will find the true depths of conviction and faith.

SOFB Community: When someone uses an author's personal non-spiritual sigils or talismans published in a book, do they tap into the sigil reservoirs of the author? Is there any connection established with the author through their use? And does the usage of these sigils or talismans contribute to feeding or depleting the author's sigil reservoirs?

Michael Lamb: Okay, that's a great question. When using sigils or talismans from an author's book, such as Franz Bardon or an occult dictionary, are you actually connected to the author in any way? Does the usage of these sigils feed or deplete the author's sigil reservoirs? I don't believe that using these sigils connects you directly to the author or affects their sigil reservoirs. If a sigil is connected to a being, it would have its own plane or dimension where the energy is relatively infinite compared to the physical plane. The sigil itself, whether created by yourself or obtained from a book, will manifest its energy in a larger-than-life manner due to its shape and dimensions.

However, if the sigil is unfamiliar or lacks strength, I might have reservations. If the sigil has a significant presence, like being carved in stone or possessing a crystalline energy that can be drawn out until it cracks the crystal, more information would be needed to assess its power. Generally, sigils obtained straight from a book may not hold as much power compared to the personal development of your own sigil. Amplifying a sigil as described in Book Two of evocational magic (PME) can enhance its potency. Thank you for the insightful question.

SOFB Community: Michael, what are your preferred methods or any recommendations for memory techniques to effectively archive, structure, and categorize our extensive experiences, associations, analogies, and other relevant information?

Michael Lamb: Well, when it comes to memory techniques for archiving and organizing our vast experiences, associations, analogies, and so on, I believe that utilizing external storage devices such as hard drives can be quite effective. Just like a hard drive stores digital information, energy also needs a place to accumulate. For instance, cathedrals, stone buildings, or even tunnels can serve as energetic storage spaces. Mind maps and mazes can be helpful tools too, as they provide a visual representation of our thoughts and energy patterns. Creating a dedicated space, whether it's an office, meditation area, or reading nook, infused with positive energy through crystals, books, and decorations, can contribute to the organization and retention of our energy and thoughts.

Archiving can be approached in various ways, using different mediums like books, vinyl records, cassettes, or video tapes. It's important to adapt to the changing times and embrace new archiving methods. Just like beings who have passed over and learned to exist in different realms and dimensions, we too must build the necessary energetic foundations to thrive in specific areas. It's akin to constructing a house, acquiring the means and creating the space to hold and maintain our energy.

Ultimately, the choice of memory techniques and archiving methods depends on personal preference and what resonates with each individual. It could be as simple as using a filing cabinet or exploring alternative approaches. The key is finding what works best for you and supports the organization and preservation of your energy and experiences.

SOFB Community: Michael, in relation to Bardon's method of astral separation and travel, assuming one possesses a strong willpower and is able to make the necessary effort to succeed consistently, are there any practices or techniques that can make the process more user-friendly and easier for the practitioner? Or is it something we simply have to become accustomed to, including the unpleasant sensations that may accompany the procedure?

Michael Lamb: Upon returning from astral travel, there are ways to lessen the unpleasantness. One approach is to explore color and sound combinations that can help create a smoother experience. There are also machines and portals available, but programming them from the 3D material realm for 4D success can be challenging. It is more effective to program them from the higher planes.

Similar to how your astral body movement may feel bumpy at first but becomes easier with practice, finding a better vehicle for transportation, such as your merkabah or light body, can help. However, it's not necessary to use those specific vehicles as there are other combinations that can be used for transportation. It's important to release any excess emotional baggage and address any imbalances or misalignments in the body, as they can disrupt the astral experience. By fine-tuning and tweaking these areas, you can achieve better stability.

In regards to balance, it's important to have a Tetra polar alignment rather than a bipolar one. This means achieving balance in the north, south, east, west, up, and down directions. You may also consider exploring the Casa Decker principle and examining platonic solids for additional insights.

SOFB Community: What is the purpose and meaning of the Buddhist Rainbow Body?

Michael Lamb: Well, here's a question that's quite complex, yet you're seeking an easy answer. The attainment of the rainbow body typically requires around 60 years of meditation, although it's possible to achieve it in shorter time periods depending on your meditation techniques. There are several books written by Rinpoche and others that delve into this topic. Over 160,000 people have reportedly attained the rainbow body across various disciplines, not just in Buddhism but also in hermetic practices.

Different traditions refer to it by various names such as the golden body, the Light Body, or the rainbow body in Buddhist terms. Essentially, it involves reaching a state where you can penetrate solid objects, leaving an imprint in solid stone. This process involves transforming atoms from particle to wave, thereby defying the laws of physics. However, it's important to note that you're not breaking these laws but rather operating on higher laws that supersede the lower ones. For instance, while gravity follows the law of levity, you need thrust and speed to counter it. It's a delicate balance between the two.

Achieving the rainbow body is akin to being awake within a dream, where you're fully aware of your dream state and can even experience another dream within the dream, similar to the concept depicted in the movie Inception. This ability has been part of our nature for thousands of years, and many individuals have attained it before. If you aspire to pursue this path, it may be beneficial to retreat from society and dedicate your life to this practice. There are numerous techniques available, but they require a lifetime commitment and deep dedication.

While I would love to provide more detailed information, there are numerous books that delve into this topic and offer in-depth explanations. Additionally, you can find accounts of monks, priests, and advanced practitioners who have attained the rainbow body. It's a phenomenon widely discussed in various philosophies and disciplines, and exploring these sources will provide you with a wealth of information. Keep in mind that in Western contexts, it may be helpful to be surrounded by nature and focus on purifying your diet and energy. Achieving the rainbow body is a significant undertaking that demands utmost commitment and discipline.

SOFB Community: Michael, how have you managed to help people in your life and the wider community?

Michael Lamb: This is a wonderful question because it allows me to reflect on the impact I've had on others. While I initially thought my influence was limited to school settings, I've come to realize that I have managed to touch the lives of many people. Without boasting, I have been able to prevent suicides and provide assistance that has extended people's lives. Through workshops and seminars, I have shared my knowledge and simplified complex concepts for the benefit of my students.

The connection I have established with the community goes beyond personal gain. I have been a source of support for my neighbors, brightening their lives when they felt bored or lost. It is difficult to fully express the extent of my impact, but I have touched many lives. I have developed deep connections with animals, crystals, and all forms of living matter, but discussing each instance would be overwhelming due to the sheer number of experiences.

What I do brings me immense joy, and I am proud of the positive changes I have facilitated in people's lives. I have been able to guide individuals who initially had limited understanding or a skewed perspective of spirituality, helping them connect with their families, loved ones, and the broader realm of knowledge. This is a blessing that I never want to cease. Additionally, I have learned to appreciate life and have played a role in protecting the lives of animals and preserving small pockets of wilderness. However, it's important to acknowledge the limitations imposed by the complexities of our world. While I strive to help as much as I can, there are certain boundaries.

Over the years, I have received valuable feedback from my students, although listing all of their experiences here would be impractical. Nevertheless, I am deeply grateful for the impact I have been able to make and for the significance this question holds for me. Thank you for asking.

SOFB: Thank you very much for your time in providing such detailed responses.

Note to readers: We had to edit some of the material to fit inside this book, that is how generous Michael has been.

GLOSSARY

What follows is a very basic glossary of terms that should help someone who is new to this subject understand more fully some of the content that is included in these interviews. It is not exhaustive and only seeks to provide a basic understanding, to fully grasp the magnitude of this work at the very least an arm chair reading of Franz Bardons three books *Initiation into Hermetics, The Practice of Magical Evocation* and *The Key to the True Kabbalah* is required and of course the practical work will further deepen understanding providing insight that is unavailable to the armchair magician.

Adam Kadmon: The primordial or archetypal man in Kabbalah, also known as the cosmic man.

Astral body: The non-physical body or "double" of a person, which is said to be capable of leaving the physical body and traveling in the astral realm.

Astral Plane: A level of existence beyond the physical world, where the astral body is said to travel.

Banishing: The act of ridding a place or person of negative energies or entities.

Binah: The third sephirah on the Kabbalistic Tree of Life, representing understanding

Chokhmah: The second sephirah on the Kabbalistic Tree of Life, representing wisdom

Conjuration: The act of summoning a spirit or entity to appear in a visible form.

Da'at: The knowledge sephirah on the Kabbalistic Tree of Life

Ein Sof: The infinite and unknowable aspect of God in Kabbalah.

Elementals: Non-physical beings that are said to inhabit the elements of earth, air, fire, and water.

Enochian: A system of magic and angelic evocation, developed by John Dee and Edward Kelley in the 16th century.

Evocation: The act of calling forth and communicating with spiritual entities, such as angels or demons.

Hermetics: A spiritual and philosophical tradition that encompasses teachings on alchemy, astrology, and the occult.

IIH: *Initiation Into Hermetics* – The first of Franz Bardons instructional manuals on Hermetics and prerequsite for further study.

Invocation: The act of calling upon a higher power or spirit for assistance or inspiration.

Kabbalah: A form of Jewish mysticism that teaches the nature of God and the creation of the universe.

Kether: The crown sephirah on the Kabbalistic Tree of Life, representing the highest aspect of God.

Magic: The use of supernatural or paranormal means to manipulate natural forces.

Magick: The additional 'k' is supposed to signify the practice of real magick versus stage magic. In this book they are used interchangeably.

Magic Circle: A circle, often drawn on the ground, that is used to protect the magician from negative energies during evocation.

Magic mirror: A mirror, often used in divination and scrying, that is believed to reveal hidden knowledge or future events.

Macrocosm: The universe, seen as a reflection of the individual person.

Malkuth: The tenth sephirah on the Kabbalistic Tree of Life, representing the physical world.

Mantra: A word or phrase, often in Sanskrit, that is repeated as a focus for meditation.

Meditation: A practice of focused concentration and self-reflection used to achieve a mentally clear and emotionally calm state.

Microcosm: The individual person, seen as a miniature representation of the universe.

Pentacle: A five-pointed star, often used in ceremonial magic, that is believed to have protective powers.

PME: *The Practice of Magical Evocation* – The second of Franz Bardons instructional manuals.

Sefirotic Tree: The diagram that represents the sephirot and their relationships in Kabbalah.

Sephirot: The ten attributes or emanations through which God creates the universe in Kabbalistic theology.

Shevirah: The breaking of the vessels, the fall of the sephirot and the creation of the material world in Kabbalah.

Sigil: A symbol, often used in ceremonial magic, that is believed to have a specific meaning or power.

Spirits: Non-physical entities that can be evoked and communicated with.

Telesmatic image: A symbol or image, often used in ceremonial magic, that is believed to represent a specific spirit or entity.

Tetragrammaton: The four-letter name of God in Hebrew, YHVH, which is considered too holy to be spoken.

KTQ: *The Key to the True Quabbalah* – The third of Franz Bardons instructional manuals.

Theosophy: A spiritual philosophy that posits the existence of an objective, intellectually comprehensible reality that is accessible to human experience.

Tzimtzum: The contraction or withdrawal of God's infinite light, creating a space for the creation of the universe in Kabbalah.

Triangle of Art: A triangle, often drawn on the ground, that is used to contain the spirit during evocation.

Transmutation: The process of transforming one substance into another, often used in reference to alchemy.

Talismans: An object, often inscribed with certain symbols or words, that is believed to have magical powers.

Yoga: A spiritual discipline that originated in ancient India, which includes physical postures, breathing exercises, and meditation.

Contact Information

- Andre Consciencia – www.Hermeticmagician.com

- Chris – www.thevoidplacesofspirit.com

- Yogic Engineering – www.yogicengineering.com

- Scott Turner – Private

- Bob from Sixty Skills – www.sixtyskills.com

- RayDel Sole – www.nextsteptomastery.com

- Sifu Mark Rasmus – www.markrasmus.com

- Wayne – Private

- Michael Lamb – www.michaelsalchemy.com

Train with the Experts

This book is the result of interviews posted on the first version of the Students of Franz Bardon blog (SOFB blog). We have now moved all interviews to a new home Perseus Arcane Academy, and removed all older interviews, the most popular of which you see in this book. Perseus Arcane Academy we see as a platform for people to share their approach, share their work and offer help and advice to those who need it. Practitioner's who feel they have something of value to teach are able to create online courses which are hosted on the site, this means that those looking for education on specific subjects can do so in a safe environment where honesty and integrity are valued over profit.

Several of those interviewed in this book now have courses over at Perseus Arcane Academy: Andre Consciencia, Sixty Skills, Ray De Sole. In addition we have other experts from both the Franz Bardon tradition and other traditions sharing their knowledge on the platform. Our aim for this platform is for it to become *the* place to go to learn about magick, evocation and kabbalah in the form of long form articles written by practitioners for practitioners or in the form of extremely detailed and practice based courses.

We hope to see you there.